MICROSOFT
Windows 2000
Brief Concepts and Techniques

Gary B. Shelly
Thomas J. Cashman
Steven G. Forsythe

COURSE TECHNOLOGY
ONE MAIN STREET
CAMBRIDGE MA 02142

Thomson Learning™

SHELLY
CASHMAN
SERIES®

Australia • Canada • Denmark • Japan • Mexico • New Zealand • Philippines
Puerto Rico • Singapore • South Africa • Spain • United Kingdom • United States

MICROSOFT

Windows 2000

Brief Concepts and Techniques

C O N T E N T S

Preface

The Shelly Cashman Series® offers the finest textbooks in computer education. The Microsoft Windows 2000 books continue with the innovation, quality, and reliability consistent with this series. We are proud that our *Microsoft Windows 3.1*, *Microsoft Windows 95*, and *Microsoft Windows 2000* books were used by more schools and more students than any other series in textbook publishing.

In our Microsoft Windows 2000 books, you will find an educationally sound and easy-to-follow pedagogy that combines a step-by-step approach with corresponding screens. The Other Ways and More About features offer in-depth knowledge of Windows 2000. The all-new project openers provide a fascinating perspective on the subject covered in the project. The Shelly Cashman Series Microsoft Windows 2000 textbooks will make your computer applications class exciting and dynamic and one that your students will remember as one of their better educational experiences.

Objectives of This Textbook

Microsoft Windows 2000: Brief Concepts and Techniques is intended for use in combination with other books in an introduction to computers or computer applications course. No computer experience is assumed. The objectives of this book are:

- To teach the fundamentals and skills necessary to adequately use Windows 2000
- To provide a knowledge base for Windows 2000 upon which students can build
- To expose students to real-world examples and procedures that will prepare them to be skilled users of Windows 2000
- To encourage independent study and help those who are working alone in a distance education environment

When students complete the course using this textbook, they will have a basic knowledge and understanding of Windows 2000.

The Shelly Cashman Approach

Features of the Shelly Cashman Series Microsoft Windows 2000 books include:

- **Project Orientation:** Related topics are presented using a project orientation that establishes a strong foundation on which students can confidently learn more advanced topics.
- **Screen-by-Screen, Step-by-Step Instructions:** Each task required to complete a project is identified throughout the development of the project. Then, steps to accomplish the task are specified and are accompanied by screens.
- **Thoroughly Tested Projects:** Every screen in the textbook is correct because it is produced by the author only after performing a step, which results in unprecedented quality.
- **Two-Page Project Openers:** Each project begins with a two-page opener that sets the tone for the project by describing an interesting aspect of Windows 2000.

Other Ways

1. Click Start button, click Run, type iexplore, click OK button
2. Press WINDOWS+R (WINDOWS key on Microsoft Natural keyboard), type iexplore, press ENTER
3. Press CTRL+ESC, press P, press I

- Other Ways Boxes for Reference: Microsoft Windows 2000 provides a variety of ways to carry out a given task. The Other Ways boxes displayed at the end of most of the step-by-step sequences specify the other ways to do the task completed in the steps. Thus, the steps and the Other Ways box make a comprehensive reference unit.

- More About Feature: These marginal annotations provide background information about the topics covered, adding interest and depth to learning.

More About

The Windows 2000 Desktop

The Windows 98 and Windows 2000 desktops are similar. Two features introduced in Windows 98, the Active Desktop and Quick Launch toolbar, remain part of the Windows 2000 desktop. The much-lauded Channel bar, designed to allow quick access to the Internet from the Windows 98 desktop, was a bomb and has been eliminated.

Organization of This Textbook

Microsoft Windows 2000: Brief Concepts and Techniques consists of two projects, as follows:

Project 1 – Fundamentals of Using Microsoft Windows 2000 Professional In Project 1, students learn about user interfaces and Windows 2000. Topics include launching Windows 2000; mouse operations; maximizing and minimizing windows; moving, sizing and scrolling windows; launching an application program; using Windows Help; and shutting down Windows 2000.

Project 2 – Using Windows Explorer In Project 2, students are introduced to Windows Explorer. Topics include displaying the contents of files, folders and drives using Explorer; expanding a drive or folder; launching an application from Explorer; copying, moving, renaming, and deleting files in Explorer.

End-of-Project Student Activities

A notable strength of the Shelly Cashman Series *Microsoft Windows 2000* textbooks is the extensive student activities at the end of each project. Well-structured student activities can make the difference between students merely participating in a class and students retaining the information they learn. These activities include:

- **What You Should Know** A listing of the tasks completed within a project together with the pages where the step-by-step, screen-by-screen explanations appear. This section provides a perfect study review for students.

- **Test Your Knowledge** Four activities designed to determine students' understanding of the material in the project. Included are true/false questions, multiple-choice questions, and two other unique activities.

- **Use Help** Users of Windows 2000 must know how to use Help. This book contains extensive Help activities. These exercises alone distinguish the Shelly Cashman Series from any other set of Windows 2000 instructional materials.

- **In the Lab** These assignments require students to make use of the knowledge gained in the project to solve problems on a computer.

- **Cases and Places** Unique case studies allow students to apply their knowledge to real-world situations. These case studies provide subjects for research papers based on information gained from a resource such as the Internet.

Shelly Cashman Series Teaching Tools

A comprehensive set of Teaching Tools accompanies this textbook in the form of a CD-ROM. The CD-ROM includes the Instructor's Manual and other teaching and testing aids. The CD-ROM (ISBN 0-7895-4469-5) is available through your Course Technology representative or by calling one of the following telephone numbers: Colleges and Universities, 1-800-648-7450; High Schools, 1-800-824-5179; Career Colleges, 1-800-477-3692; Canada, 1-800-268-2222; and Corporations and Government Agencies, 1-800-340-7450. The contents of the CD-ROM follow.

- **Instructor's Manual** The Instructor's Manual is made up of Microsoft Word files that include lecture notes, solutions to laboratory assignments, and a large test bank. The files allow you to modify the lecture notes or generate quizzes and exams from the test bank using your own word processing software. Where appropriate, solutions to laboratory assignments are embedded as icons.

- **Figures in the Book** Illustrations for every screen in the textbook are available. Use this ancillary to create a slide show from the illustrations for lecture or to print transparencies for use in lecture with an overhead projector.

- **Course Test Manager** Course Test Manager is a powerful testing and assessment package that enables instructors to create and print tests from the large test bank. Instructors with access to a networked computer lab (LAN) can administer, grade, and track tests online.

- **Interactive Labs** Eighteen hands-on interactive labs solidify and reinforce computer concepts.

Shelly Cashman Online

Shelly Cashman Online is a World Wide Web service available to instructors and students of computer education. Visit Shelly Cashman Online at www.scseries.com. Shelly Cashman Online is divided into four areas:

- **Series Information** Information on the Shelly Cashman Series products.

- **Teaching Resources** Designed for instructors teaching from and using Shelly Cashman Series textbooks and software. This area includes password-protected instructor materials that can be downloaded, course outlines, teaching tips, and much more.

- **Community** Opportunities to discuss your course and your ideas with instructors in your field and with the Shelly Cashman Series team.

- **Student Center** Dedicated to students learning about computers with Shelly Cashman Series textbooks and software. This area includes cool links, data that can be downloaded, and much more.

Acknowledgments

The Shelly Cashman Series would not be the leading computer education series without the contributions of outstanding publishing professionals. First, and foremost, among them is Becky Herrington, director of production and designer. She is the heart and soul of the Shelly Cashman Series, and it is only through her leadership, dedication, and tireless efforts that superior products are made possible. Becky created and produced the award-winning Windows series of books.

Under Becky's direction, the following individuals made significant contributions to these books: Doug Cowley, production manager; Ginny Harvey, series specialist and developmental editor; Ken Russo, senior Web designer; Mike Bodnar, associate production manager; Mark Norton, Web designer; Meena Mohtadi, production editor; Chris Schneider, graphic artist and cover designer; Hector Arvizu, Kathy Mayers, and Christy Pardini, graphic artists; Jeanne Black and Betty Hopkins, Quark experts; Nancy Lamm, copyeditor; Marilyn Martin, proofreader; and Laurie Sullivan, contributing writer.

Special thanks go to Richard Keaveny, managing editor; Jim Quasney, series consulting editor; Lora Wade, product manager; Erin Bennett, associate product manager; Francis Schurgot, Web product manager; Marc Ouellette, associate Web product manager; Rajika Gupta, product marketing manager; and Erin Runyon, editorial assistant.

Gary B. Shelly
Thomas J. Cashman
Steven G. Forsythe

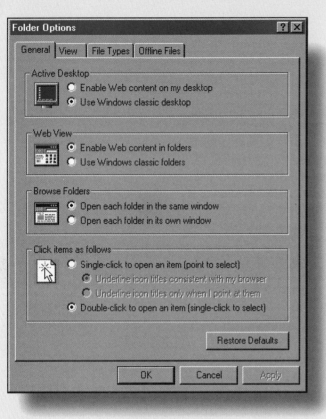

FIGURE 1

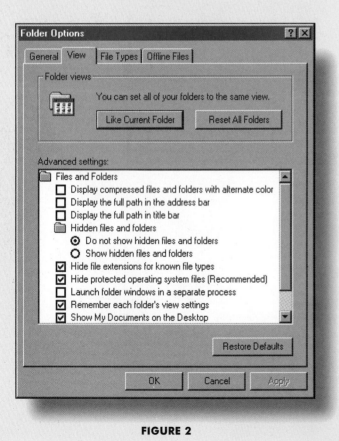

FIGURE 2

Instructions for Restoring the Default Folder Options Settings

The projects and assignments in this textbook are presented using the default folder options settings, as chosen by Microsoft Corporation. To ensure your success in completing the projects and assignments, you must install the Windows 2000 Professional operating system on your computer system and restore the folder options settings. The following steps illustrate how to restore the default folder options settings.

1. Double-click the My Computer icon on the desktop.
2. Click Tools on the My Computer menu bar.
3. Click the Folder Options command on the Tools menu to display the Folder Options dialog box (Figure 1).
4. If necessary, click the General tab in the Folder Options dialog box to display the General sheet.
5. On a piece of paper, write down the name of each folder option that is selected in the General sheet in the Folder Options dialog box.
6. Click the Restore Defaults button in the General sheet.
7. Click the View tab to display the View sheet (Figure 2).
8. On a piece of paper, write down the name of each advanced setting that is selected in the View sheet in the Folder Options dialog box.
9. Click the Restore Defaults button in the View sheet.
10. Click the OK button in the Folder Options dialog box.

As a result of restoring the default folder option settings, you can perform the steps and assignments in each project of this book. If, after finishing the steps and assignments, you must restore the folder options to their original settings, perform steps 1 through 4 above, click the option button of each setting you wrote down in step 5, perform step 7 above, click the check box and option button of each setting you wrote down in step 8, and then perform step 10.

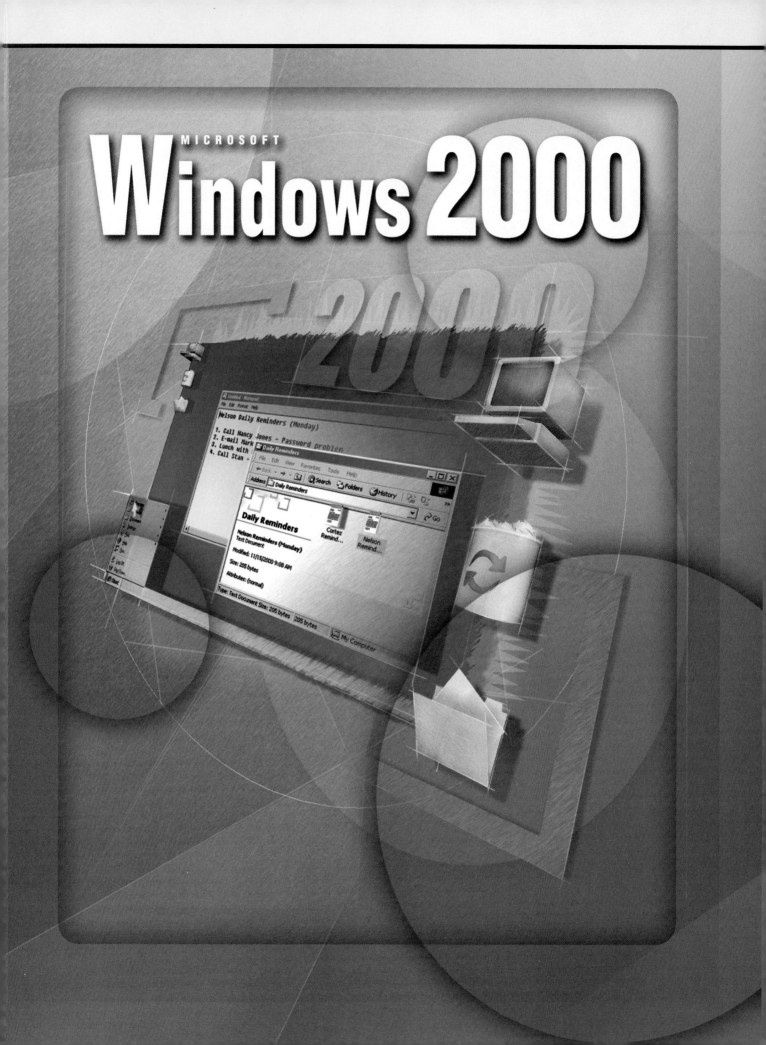

Microsoft **Windows 2000**

PROJECT

1

Microsoft Windows 2000

Fundamentals of Using Microsoft Windows 2000 Professional

OBJECTIVES

You will have mastered the material in this project when you can:

- Describe the Microsoft Windows 2000 operating system family
- Explain operating system, server, workstation, and user interface
- Identify the objects on the Microsoft Windows 2000 desktop
- Perform the basic mouse operations: point, click, right-click, double-click, drag, and right-drag
- Open, minimize, maximize, restore, and close a Windows 2000 window
- Move and size a window on the Windows 2000 desktop
- Scroll in a window
- Understand keyboard shortcut notation
- Launch an application program
- Use Windows 2000 Help
- Shut down Windows 2000

Windows 2000

Leads the Way in the New Millennium

In the twenty-first century, the Microsoft Windows 2000 operating system leads the way with its advanced and improved software technology, making it easier, more cost-effective, and enjoyable for people and businesses to use computers. Microsoft Corporation under the leadership of Bill Gates has been a continuous source of innovative products.

Bill Gates's computing efforts began when he was in grade school, when he and classmate, Paul Allen, learned the BASIC programming language from a manual and programmed a mainframe computer using a Teletype terminal they purchased with the proceeds from a rummage sale. In high school, Gates and Allen had a thirst for more computing power. They wrote custom programs for local businesses during the summer and split their $5,000 salaries between cash and computer time. They also debugged software problems at local businesses in return for computer use.

In Gates's sophomore year, one of his teachers asked him to teach his computer skills to his classmates. In 1972, Gates and Allen read an article in *Electronics* magazine about Intel's first microprocessor chip. They requested a manual from Intel, developed a device that experimented with pushing the chip to its limits, and formed the Traf-O-Data company, an endeavor that ultimately would lead to the formation of something much larger.

In 1973, Gates entered Harvard and Allen landed a programming job with Honeywell.

They continued to communicate and scheme about the power of computers when, in 1975, the Altair 8800 computer showed up on the cover of *Popular Electronics*. This computer was about the size of the Traf-O-Data device and contained a new Intel computer chip. At that point, they knew they were going into business. Gates left Harvard and Allen left Honeywell

When they formed Microsoft in 1975, the company had three programmers, one product, and revenues of $16,000. The founders had no business plan, no capital, and no financial backing, but they did have a product – a form of the BASIC programming language tailored for the first microcomputer.

In 1980, IBM approached Microsoft and asked the company to provide an operating system for its new IBM personal computer. The deadline? Three months. Gates purchased the core of a suitable operating system, dubbed Q-DOS (Quick and Dirty Operating System). Microsoft's version, MS-DOS, would become the international standard for IBM and IBM-compatible personal computers. Riding the meteoric rise in sales of IBM-compatible computers and attendant sales of MS-DOS, Microsoft continued to improve its software stream of revisions. At a significant branch of the family tree, Windows made it debut, providing an intuitive graphical user interface (GUI). Similarly, Windows 95, Windows 98, and Windows NT provided further advances.

The Microsoft Windows 2000 operating system family expands the possibilities even further with the Windows 2000 Server, Windows 2000 Advanced Server, and Windows 2000 Data Center designed for use on a server in a computer network. The Windows 2000 Professional can be used on computer workstations and portable computers. As you will learn as you complete the projects in this book, you can control the computer and communicate with other computers on a network. In the networked society of the new millennium, Windows 2000 leads the way.

Microsoft Windows 2000

Fundamentals of Using Microsoft Windows 2000 Professional

P R O J E C T

1

C A S E   P E R S P E C T I V E

After weeks of planning, your organization finally installed Microsoft Windows 2000 Advanced Server edition on their server and Microsoft Windows 2000 Professional on all workstations. As the computer trainer for the upcoming in-house seminar, you realize you should know more about Microsoft Windows 2000 Professional but have had little time to learn about it. Since installing Windows 2000 Professional, many employees have come to you with questions. You have taken the time to answer their questions by sitting down with them at their computers and searching for the answers using the Microsoft Help feature.

From their questions, you determine that you should customize the seminar to cover the basics of Windows 2000 Professional, including basic mouse operations, working with windows, launching an application, and searching for answers to their questions using Windows 2000 Help. Your goal is to become familiar with Microsoft Windows 2000 Professional in order to teach the seminar effectively to participants.

Introduction

An **operating system** is the set of computer instructions, called a computer program, that controls the allocation of computer hardware such as memory, disk devices, printers, and CD-ROM and DVD drives, and provides the capability for you to communicate with the computer. The most popular and widely used operating system for personal computers is **Microsoft Windows**. The most powerful of the Microsoft Windows operating systems, **Microsoft Windows 2000**, is designed for business users.

Microsoft Windows 2000 Operating System Family

The Microsoft Windows 2000 family of operating systems consists of the Microsoft Windows 2000 Server, Microsoft Windows 2000 Advanced Server, Microsoft Windows 2000 Data Center, and Microsoft Windows 2000 Professional.

The Microsoft Windows 2000 Server, Microsoft Windows 2000 Advanced Server, and Microsoft Windows 2000 Data Center operating systems are designed for use on a server in a computer network. A **server** is a computer that controls access to the hardware and software on a network and provides a centralized storage area for programs, data, and information. The complexity of the network determines which operating system runs on the server. Figure 1-1 illustrates a simple computer network consisting of a server, three computers (called workstations), and a laser printer connected to the server (Figure 1-1).

The choice of which operating system to use on a server depends on the requirements of an organization and the complexity of its computer network. The **Microsoft Windows 2000 Server edition** is an operating system ideal for small to

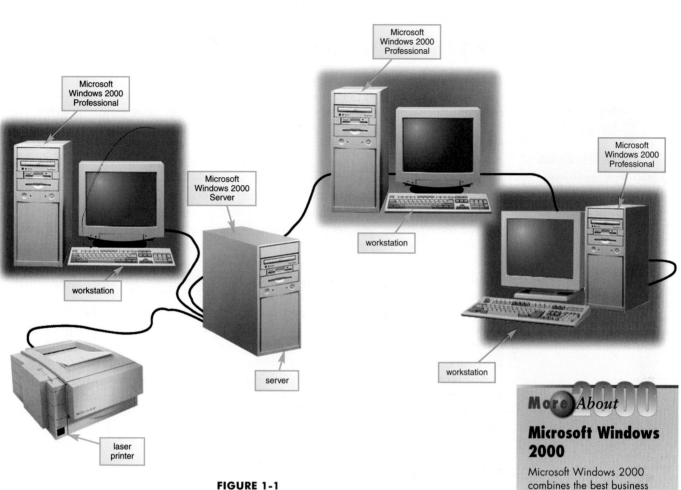

FIGURE 1-1

medium-sized organizations with numerous workgroups and branch offices. The **Microsoft Windows 2000 Advanced Server edition** is a more powerful mid-range operating system for use with larger organizations that run demanding applications such as e-commerce, have corporate Internet and intranet sites, and perform database-intensive work. Microsoft Windows 2000 Advanced Server edition improves the performance of the network by allowing the server to run up to four processors and use larger amounts of memory than the Microsoft Windows 2000 Server edition.

The **Microsoft Windows 2000 Data Center edition** is the most powerful operating system produced by Microsoft and meets the needs of businesses and Internet Service Provider (ISP) organizations with large scale Internet and intranet operations. This edition allows the server to run up to 16 processors. Because the network illustrated in Figure 1-1 is relatively simple, the Microsoft Windows 2000 Server operating system is chosen to run on the server.

Microsoft Windows 2000 Professional is the operating system designed for use on computer workstations and portable computers. A **workstation** is a computer connected to a server. In Figure 1-1, the operating system installed on the three workstations is Microsoft Windows 2000 Professional.

This book demonstrates how to use Microsoft Windows 2000 Professional to control the computer and communicate with other computers on a network. In Project 1, you will learn about Windows 2000 and how to use the Windows 2000 user interface.

Microsoft Windows 2000

Microsoft Windows 2000 combines the best business features of Windows 98 with the strengths of Windows NT 4.0. Windows 98, designed for use on personal computers, is the most popular operating system for personal computers. Windows NT 4.0, designed for use on a computer network, is the most widely used version of Windows NT.

Microsoft Windows 2000

A vast amount of information about Microsoft Windows 2000 is available on the Internet. For additional information about Microsoft Windows 2000, launch the Internet Explorer browser (see pages WIN 1.32 thru WIN 1.35), type www.scsite.com/win2000/more.htm in the Address box in the Microsoft Internet Explorer window, and then press the ENTER key.

Microsoft Windows 2000 Professional

Microsoft Windows 2000 Professional (called **Windows 2000** for the rest of this book) is an operating system that performs every function necessary for you to communicate with and control your computer and access information on other workstations on the network. Windows 2000 is called a **32-bit operating system** because it uses 32 bits for addressing and other purposes, which means the operating system can address more than four gigabytes of RAM (random-access memory) and perform tasks faster than older operating systems.

Windows 2000 includes **Microsoft Internet Explorer** (**IE**), a software program developed by Microsoft Corporation, that integrates the Windows 2000 desktop and the Internet. The **Internet** is a worldwide group of connected computer networks that allows public access to information on thousands of subjects and gives users the ability to send messages and obtain products and services. Internet Explorer allows you to work with programs and files in a similar fashion, whether they are located on your computer, a local network, or the Internet.

Windows 2000 is easy to use and can be customized to fit individual needs. Windows 2000 simplifies the process of working with documents and applications by transferring data between documents, organizing the manner in which you interact with the computer, and using the computer to access information on the Internet and/or intranet. Windows 2000 is used to run **application programs**, which are programs that perform an application-related function such as word processing. To use the application programs that can be executed under Windows 2000, you must know about the Windows 2000 user interface.

What Is a User Interface?

A **user interface** is the combination of hardware and software that you use to communicate with and control the computer. Through the user interface, you are able to make selections on the computer, request information from the computer, and respond to messages displayed by the computer. Thus, a user interface provides the means for dialogue between you and the computer.

Hardware and software together form the user interface. Among the hardware devices associated with a user interface are the monitor, keyboard, and mouse (Figure 1-2). The **monitor** displays messages and provides information. You respond by entering data in the form of a command or other response using the **keyboard** or **mouse**. Among the responses available to you are responses that specify which application program to run, what document to open, when to print, and where to store data for future use.

The computer software associated with the user interface consists of the programs that engage you in dialogue (Figure 1-2). The computer software determines the messages you receive, the manner in which you should respond, and the actions that occur based on your responses.

The goal of an effective user interface is to be **user friendly**, which means the software can be used easily by individuals with limited training. Research studies have indicated that the use of graphics can play an important role in aiding users to interact effectively with a computer. A **graphical user interface**, or **GUI** (pronounced gooey), is a user interface that displays graphics in addition to text when it communicates with the user.

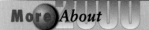

More About

Microsoft Windows 2000 Professional

For additional information about Windows 2000 Professional, launch the Internet Explorer browser (see pages WIN 1.32 thru WIN 1.35), type www.scsite.com/ win2000/more.htm in the Address box in the Microsoft Internet Explorer window, and then press the ENTER key.

More About

The Windows 2000 Interface

Some older interfaces, called command-line interfaces, required that you type keywords (special words, phrases, or codes the computer understands) or press special keys on the keyboard to communicate with the interface. Today, graphical user interfaces incorporate colorful graphics, use of the mouse, and Web browser-like features, making today's interfaces user-friendly.

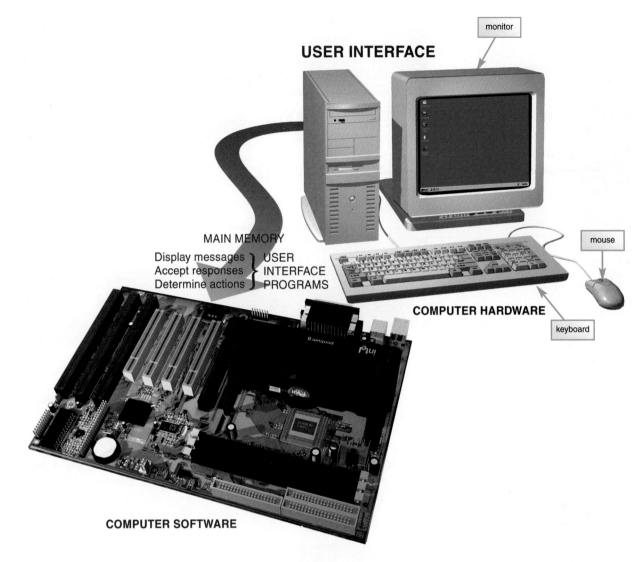

FIGURE 1-2

The Windows 2000 graphical user interface was designed carefully to be easier to set up, simpler to learn, faster and more powerful, and better integrated with the Internet than previous versions of Microsoft Windows.

Launching Microsoft Windows 2000

When you turn on the computer, an introductory screen containing the words, Microsoft Windows 2000 Professional, and the Please Wait... screen display momentarily followed by the Welcome to Windows dialog box (Figure 1-3 on the next page). A **dialog box** displays whenever Windows 2000 needs to supply information to you or wants you to enter information or select among several options. The **title bar**, which is at the top of the dialog box and blue in color, identifies the name of the dialog box (Welcome to Windows). The Welcome to Windows dialog box displays on a blue background and contains the Windows logo, title (Microsoft Windows 2000 Professional Built on NT Technology), keyboard icon, instructions (Press Ctrl-Alt-Delete to begin.), a message, and the Help link.

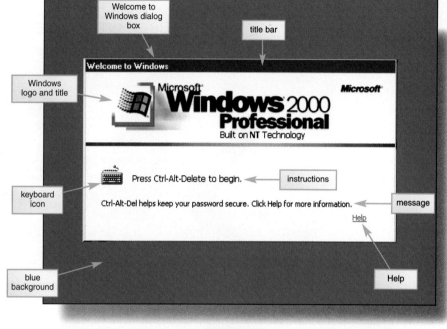

FIGURE 1-3

User Names and Passwords

A unique user name identifies each user. Users often use a variation of their name as the user name. For example, Ron Woodward might choose ronwoodward or rwoodword. A password is a combination of characters that allow you access to certain computer resources on the network. Passwords should be kept confidential.

Holding down the CTRL key and pressing the ALT and DELETE keys simultaneously will remove the Welcome to Windows dialog box and display the Log On to Windows dialog box (Figure 1-4). The Log On to Windows dialog box contains the User name and Password text boxes, Log on to box, Log on using dial-up connection check box, and four command buttons (OK, Cancel, Shutdown, and Options). A **text box** is a rectangular area in which you can enter text. Currently, the user name (Brad Wilson) displays in the User name text box, a series of asterisks (*****) displays in the Password text box to hide the password entered by the user, and the computer name, BRADWILSON (this computer), displays in the Log on to box. The **check box** represents an option to log on using an established dial-up Internet connection. The **command buttons** allow you to perform different operations, such as accepting the user name and password or displaying additional options. If you do not know your user name or password, ask your instructor.

Entering your user name in the User name text box and your password in the Password text box and then clicking the OK button will clear the screen and allow several items to display on a background called the **desktop**. The default color of the desktop background is blue, but your computer may display a different color.

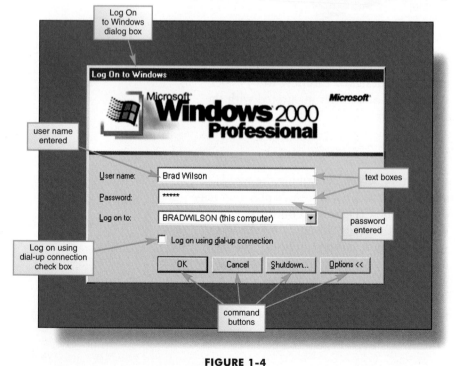

FIGURE 1-4

The items on the desktop shown in Figure 1-5 include five icons and their names on the left side of the desktop and the taskbar at the bottom of the desktop. Using the five **icons**, you can store documents in one location (**My Documents**), view the contents of the computer (**My Computer**), work with other computers connected to the computer (**My Network Places**), discard unneeded objects (**Recycle Bin**), and browse Web pages on the Internet (**Internet Explorer**). Your computer's desktop may contain more, fewer, or different icons because you can customize the desktop of the computer.

The **taskbar** shown at the bottom of the screen in Figure 1-5 contains the Start button, Quick Launch toolbar, taskbar button area, and status area. The **Start button** allows you to launch a program quickly, find or open a document, change the computer's settings, shut down the computer, and perform many more tasks. The **Quick Launch toolbar** contains three icons. The first icon allows you to view an uncluttered desktop at any time (**Show Desktop**). The second icon launches Internet Explorer (**Launch Internet Explorer Browser**). The third icon launches Outlook Express (**Launch Outlook Express**).

More About

The Windows 2000 Desktop

The Windows 98 and Windows 2000 desktops are similar. Two features introduced in Windows 98, the Active Desktop and Quick Launch toolbar, remain part of the Windows 2000 desktop. The much-lauded Channel bar, designed to allow quick access to the Internet from the Windows 98 desktop, was a bomb and has been eliminated.

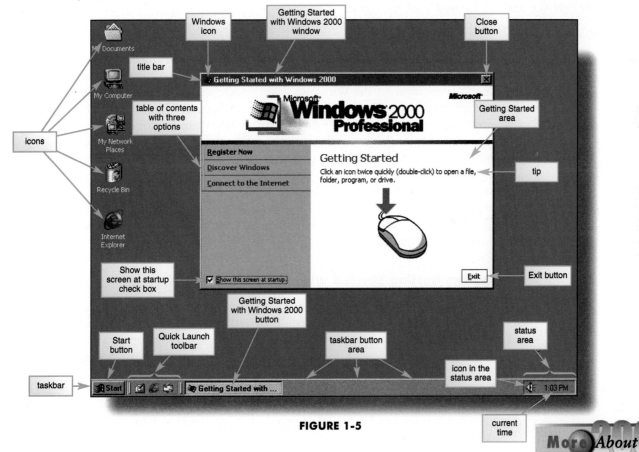

FIGURE 1-5

The **taskbar button area** contains buttons to indicate which windows are open on the desktop. In Figure 1-5, the Getting Started with Windows 2000 window displays on the desktop and the Getting Started with Windows 2000 button displays in the taskbar button area. The **status area** contains a **speaker icon** to adjust the computer's volume level. The status area also displays the current time (1:03 PM). The status area on your desktop may contain more, fewer, or some different icons because the contents of the status area can change.

More About

The Contents of the Desktop

Because Windows 2000 can be easily customized, your desktop may not resemble the desktop in Figure 1-5. For example, the icon titles on the desktop may be underlined or objects not shown in Figure 1-5 may display on your desktop. If this is the case, contact your instructor to change the desktop.

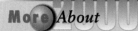

The Getting Started with Windows 2000 Window

If the Getting Started window does not display and you want the window to display, click the Start button on the taskbar, click Run on the Start menu, type welcome in the Open text box, and click the OK button.

The Getting Started with Windows 2000 window that may display on the desktop when you launch Windows 2000 is shown in Figure 1-5 on the previous page. The title bar (dark blue) contains the Windows icon, identifies the name of the window (Getting Started with Windows 2000), and contains the Close button, which you can use to close the window. The **Getting Started with Windows 2000 button** in the taskbar button area indicates the Getting Started with Windows 2000 window displays on the desktop. The ellipsis on the button indicates the button name (Getting Started with Windows 2000) is abbreviated on the button.

In the Getting Started with Windows 2000 window, a table of contents containing three options (Register Now, Discover Windows, and Connect to the Internet) and the Getting Started area containing constantly changing helpful tips about Windows 2000 display. The options in the table of contents allow you to perform different tasks such as registering the Windows 2000 operating system, learning Windows 2000 using the Discover Windows 2000 tour, and connecting to the Internet. Pointing to an option in the table of contents replaces the contents of the Getting Started area with an explanation of the option. Clicking an option begins the task associated with the option.

A check box containing a check mark displays below the table of contents. The check mark in the check box represents an option to display the Getting Started with Windows 2000 window each time you launch Windows 2000. The **Exit button** at the bottom of the Getting Started area closes the window.

Nearly every item on the Windows 2000 desktop is considered an object. Even the desktop itself is an object. Every **object** has properties. The **properties** of an object are unique to that specific object and may affect what can be done to the object or what the object does. For example, the properties of an object may be the color of the object, such as the color of the desktop.

In the lower-right of the desktop is the mouse pointer. On the desktop, the **mouse pointer** is the shape of a block arrow. The mouse pointer allows you to point to objects on the desktop and may change shape when it points to different objects. A shadow may display behind the mouse pointer to make the mouse pointer display in a three-dimensional form.

Closing the Getting Started with Windows 2000 Window

As noted, the Getting Started with Windows 2000 window may display when you launch Windows 2000. If the Getting Started with Windows 2000 window does display on the desktop, normally you should close it before beginning any other operations using Windows 2000. To close the window, complete the following step.

TO CLOSE THE GETTING STARTED WITH WINDOWS 2000 WINDOW

1 Hold down the ALT key on the keyboard, press the F4 key on the keyboard, and then release the ALT key.

The Getting Started with Windows 2000 window closes.

The Desktop as a Work Area

The Windows 2000 desktop and the objects on the desktop emulate a work area in an office. You may think of the Windows desktop as an electronic version of the top of your desk. You can move objects around on the desktop, look at them and then put them aside, and so on. In Project 1, you will learn how to interact with and communicate with the Windows 2000 desktop.

Communicating with Windows 2000

The Windows 2000 interface provides the means for dialogue between you and the computer. Part of this dialogue involves your requesting information from the computer and responding to messages displayed by the computer. You can request information and respond to messages using either a mouse or a keyboard.

Mouse Operations

A **mouse** is a pointing device used with Windows 2000 that is attached to the computer by a cable. Although not required to use Windows 2000, Windows supports the use of the **Microsoft IntelliMouse** (Figure 1-6). The IntelliMouse contains three buttons, the primary mouse button, the secondary mouse button, and the wheel button between the primary and secondary mouse buttons. Typically, the **primary mouse button** is the left mouse button and the **secondary mouse button** is the right mouse button although Windows 2000 allows you to switch them. In this book, the left mouse button is the primary mouse button and the right mouse button is the secondary mouse button. The functions the **wheel button** and wheel perform depend on the software application being used. If the mouse connected to the computer is not an IntelliMouse, it will not have a wheel button between the primary and secondary mouse buttons.

Using the mouse, you can perform the following operations: (1) point; (2) click; (3) right-click; (4) double-click; (5) drag; and (6) right-drag. These operations are demonstrated on the following pages.

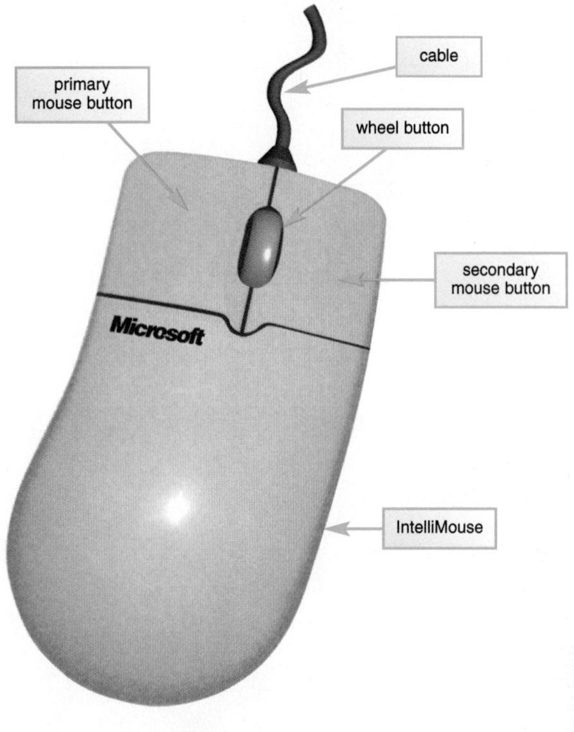

primary mouse button

cable

wheel button

secondary mouse button

IntelliMouse

FIGURE 1-6

single ball on underside of mouse

FIGURE 1-7

Point and Click

Point means you move the mouse across a flat surface until the mouse pointer rests on the item of choice on the desktop. As you move the mouse across a flat surface, Windows 2000 senses the movement of a ball on the underside of the mouse (Figure 1-7), and the mouse pointer moves across the desktop in the same direction.

Click means you press and release the primary mouse button, which in this book is the left mouse button. In most cases, you must point to an item before you click. To become acquainted with the use of the mouse, perform the steps on the next page to point to and click various objects on the desktop.

 To Point and Click

① **Point to the Start button on the taskbar by moving the mouse across a flat surface until the mouse pointer rests on the Start button.**

*The mouse pointer on the Start button displays a **ToolTip** (Click here to begin) (Figure 1-8). The ToolTip, which provides instructions, displays on the desktop for approximately five seconds.*

My Documents

My Computer

My Network Places

Recycle Bin

Internet Explorer

Start button

ToolTip

Click here to begin

🔀 Start

mouse pointer

1:05 PM

FIGURE 1-8

② **Click the Start button by pressing and releasing the left mouse button.**

*The **Start menu** displays and the Start button is recessed (Figure 1-9). A **menu** is a list of related commands. A **command** performs a specific action, such as obtaining help. Each command consists of an icon and a name. A **right arrow** follows some commands to indicate pointing to the command will display a submenu. An **ellipsis** (...) indicates more information is required to execute a command.*

icon

command name

Windows Update

New Office Document

Open Office Document

Start menu

Programs

Documents

Settings

Search

right arrows

Help

Run...

ellipsis

Shut Down...

commands display in three sections

Help command

🔀 Start

Start button recessed

1:05 PM

FIGURE 1-9

3 **Point to Programs on the Start menu.**

*When you point to Programs, Windows 2000 highlights the Programs command on the Start menu and the **Programs submenu** displays (Figure 1-10). A **submenu** is a menu that displays when you point to a command followed by a right arrow. Whenever you point to a command on a menu, the command is highlighted.*

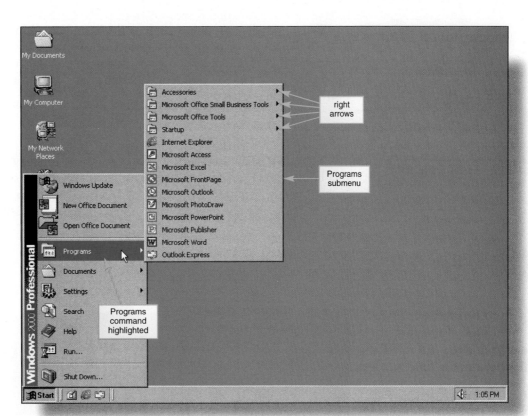

FIGURE 1-10

4 **Point to an open area of the desktop and then click the open area of the desktop.**

The Start menu and Programs submenu close (Figure 1-11). The mouse pointer points to the desktop. To close a menu anytime, click any open area of the desktop except on the menu itself. The Start button is no longer recessed.

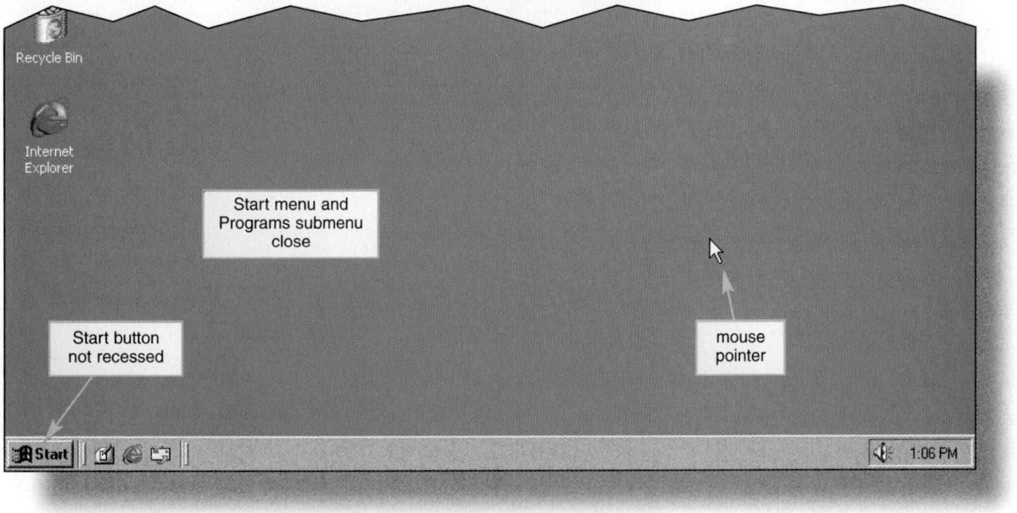

FIGURE 1-11

The Start menu shown in Figure 1-9 contains three sections. The top section contains commands to launch the Windows Update application (Windows Update), create or open a Microsoft Office document (New Office Document and Open Office Document); the middle section contains commands to launch an application, work with documents, customize options, and search for files or help (Programs, Documents, Settings, Search, Help, and Run); and the bottom section contains the command to shut down Windows 2000 (Shut Down).

The Right Mouse

The earliest versions of Microsoft Windows made little use of the right mouse button. In Windows 2000, the right mouse button makes it easy to display a list of commands for an object (called a shortcut menu) and to copy and move objects on the desktop.

When you click an object such as the Start button in Figure 1-9 on page WIN 1.14, you must point to the object before you click. In the steps that follow, the instruction that directs you to point to a particular item and then click is, Click the particular item. For example, Click the Start button means point to the Start button and then click.

Right-Click

Right-click means you press and release the secondary mouse button, which in this book is the right mouse button. As directed when using the primary mouse button for clicking an object, normally you will point to an object before you right-click it. Perform the following steps to right-click the desktop.

 To Right-Click

① Point to an open area of the desktop and then press and release the right mouse button.

A shortcut menu displays (Figure 1-12). Right-clicking an object, such as the desktop, displays a **shortcut menu** *that contains commands specifically for use with that object. When a command on a menu appears dimmed, such as the Paste or Paste Shortcut commands, that command is unavailable.*

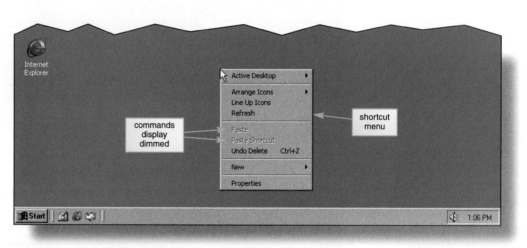

FIGURE 1-12

② Point to New on the shortcut menu.

When you point to the New command, Windows 2000 highlights the New command and displays the New sub-menu (Figure 1-13). The number of commands and the actual commands that display on your computer may be different.

③ Click an open area of the desktop to remove the shortcut menu and the New submenu.

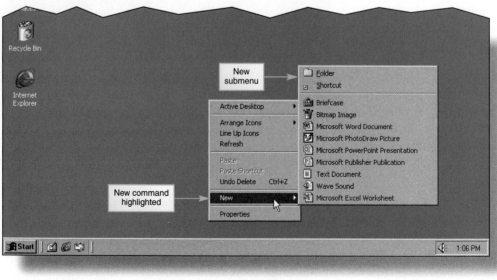

FIGURE 1-13

Whenever you right-click an object, a shortcut menu will display. As you will see, the use of shortcut menus speeds up your work and adds flexibility to your interaction with the computer.

Double-Click

Double-click means you quickly press and release the left mouse button twice without moving the mouse. In most cases, you must point to an item before you double-click. Perform the following step to open the My Computer window on the desktop by double-clicking the My Computer icon.

More About

Double-Clicking

Double-clicking is the most difficult mouse skill to learn. Many people have a tendency to move the mouse before they click a second time, even when they do not want to move the mouse. You should find, however, that with a little practice, double-clicking becomes quite natural.

Steps To Open a Window by Double-Clicking

1 Point to the My Computer icon on the desktop and then double-click by quickly pressing and releasing the left mouse button twice without moving the mouse.

The My Computer window opens and the recessed My Computer button displays in the taskbar button area (Figure 1-14). The My Computer window allows you to view the contents of the computer.

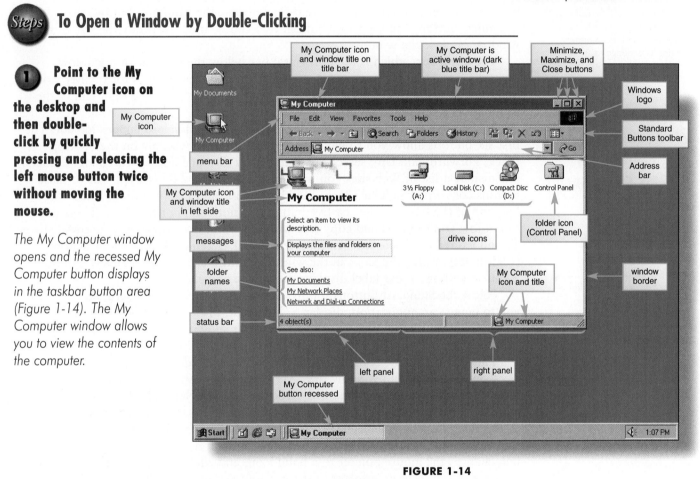

FIGURE 1-14

The My Computer window, the only open window, is the active window. The **active window** is the window you currently are using or that currently is selected. Whenever you click an object that can be opened, such as the My Computer icon, Windows 2000 will open the object; and a recessed button in the taskbar button area will identify the open object. The recessed button identifies the active window.

The contents of the My Computer window on your computer may be different from the contents of the My Computer window shown in Figure 1-14.

My Computer

While the trade press and media once poked fun at the My Computer icon name, Microsoft continues to expand on the concept. Microsoft added the My Documents icon to the Windows 98 desktop and replaced the Network Neighborhood icon with the My Network Places icon on the Windows 2000 desktop. Microsoft still contends that beginners find these names easier to understand.

The Contents of the My Computer Window

Because windows are easily customized, your My Computer window may not resemble the window in Figure 1-14 on the previous page. For example, different toolbars may display, icons may display smaller, or the panels may not display. If this is the case, contact your instructor to change the contents the My Computer window.

The My Computer Window

The thin line, or **window border**, surrounding the My Computer window shown in Figure 1-14 on the previous page determines its shape and size. The **title bar** at the top of the window contains a small icon that is the same as the icon on the desktop and the **window title** (My Computer) that identifies the window. The color of the title bar (dark blue) and the recessed My Computer button in the taskbar button area indicate the My Computer window is the active window. The color of the active window on your computer may be different from the dark blue color shown in Figure 1-14.

Clicking the icon at the left on the title bar will display the **System menu**, which contains commands to carry out the actions associated with the My Computer window. At the right on the title bar are three buttons, the Minimize button, the Maximize button, and the Close button, that can be used to specify the size of the window or close the window.

The **menu bar**, which is the horizontal bar below the title bar of a window (Figure 1-14 on the previous page), contains a list of menu names for the My Computer window: File, Edit, View, Favorites, Tools, and Help. At the right end of the menu bar is a button containing the Windows logo.

Below the menu bar, eleven buttons display on the **Standard Buttons toolbar**. The first six buttons allow you to navigate through an open window on the desktop (Back, Forward, and Up); search for and display files or folders (Search and Folders); and display a list of Web sites you previously have visited (History). Four of these buttons contain a **text label** (Back, Search, Folders, and History) that identify the function of the button. The last five buttons do not contain text labels. These buttons allow you to move and copy text within a window or between windows (Move To and Copy To); delete text within a window (Delete); undo a previous action (Undo); and display the icons in the window in different formats (Views). Pointing to a button without a text label displays the button name.

Below the Standard Buttons toolbar is the Address bar. The **Address bar** allows you to launch an application, display a document, open another window, and search for information on the Internet. The Address bar shown in Figure 1-14 on the previous page contains the My Computer icon and window title.

The area below the Standard Buttons toolbar is divided into two panels. The My Computer icon and window title, My Computer, display in the left panel. Several messages and three folder names (My Documents, My Network Places, and Network and Dial-Up Connections) display below the icon and title in the left panel. The three folder names are underlined and display in blue font. Underlined text, such as the folder names, is referred to as a **hyperlink**, or simply a **link**. Pointing to a hyperlink changes the mouse pointer to a hand icon, and clicking a hyperlink displays the contents of the associated folder in the window. Because the My Computer window is divided into two panels and the left panel contains hyperlinks, the window is said to display in the **Web view**.

The right panel of the My Computer window contains four icons. A title below each icon identifies the icon. The first three icons, called **drive icons**, represent a 3½ Floppy (A:) drive, a Local Disk (C:) drive, and a Compact Disc (D:) drive. The fourth icon is the Control Panel folder. A **folder** is an object created to contain related documents, applications, and other folders. A folder in Windows 2000 contains items in much the same way a folder on your desk contains items. The **Control Panel folder** allows you to personalize the computer, such as specifying how you want the desktop to look.

Clicking a drive or folder icon selects the icon in the right panel and displays information about the drive or folder in the left panel. Double-clicking a drive or folder icon displays the contents of the corresponding drive or folder in the right panel and information about the drive or folder in the left panel. You may find more, fewer, or different drive and folder icons in the My Computer window on your computer.

A message at the left on the **status bar** located at the bottom of the window indicates the right panel contains four objects (see Figure 1-14 on page WIN 1.17). The My Computer icon and title display to the right of the message on the status bar.

Minimize Button

Two buttons on the title bar of a window, the Minimize button and the Maximize button, allow you to control the way a window displays or does not display on the desktop. When you click the **Minimize button** (see Figure 1-14 on page WIN 1.17), the My Computer window no longer displays on the desktop and the recessed My Computer button in the taskbar button area changes to a non-recessed button. A minimized window still is open but it does not display on the screen. To minimize and then redisplay the My Computer window, complete these steps.

More About 2000

Minimizing Windows

Windows management on the Windows 2000 desktop is important in order to keep the desktop uncluttered. You will find yourself frequently minimizing windows and then later reopening them with a click of a button in the taskbar button area.

 Steps **To Minimize and Redisplay a Window**

① **Point to the Minimize button on the title bar of the My Computer window.**

The mouse pointer points to the Minimize button on the My Computer window title bar (Figure 1-15). A ToolTip displays below the Minimize button and the My Computer button in the taskbar button area is recessed.

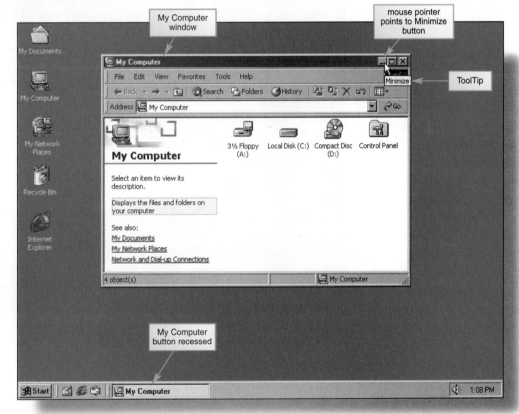

FIGURE 1-15

Click the Minimize button.

When you minimize the My Computer window, Windows 2000 removes the My Computer window from the desktop and the My Computer button changes to a non-recessed button (Figure 1-16).

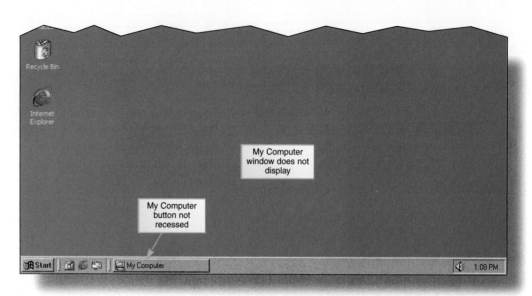

FIGURE 1-16

③ Click the My Computer button in the taskbar button area.

The My Computer window displays on the desktop in the same place and size it was before being minimized (Figure 1-17). In addition, the My Computer window is the active window because it contains the dark blue title bar, and the My Computer button in the taskbar button area is recessed.

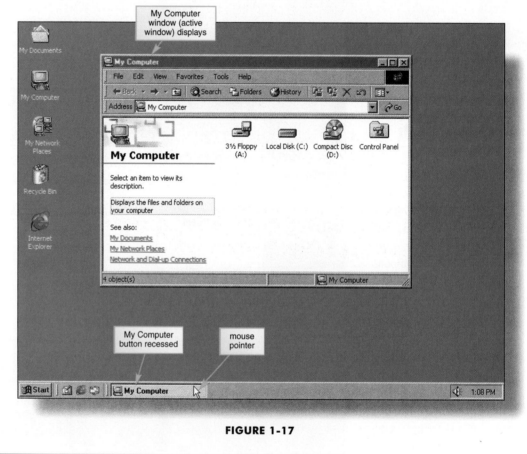

FIGURE 1-17

Whenever a window is minimized, it does not display on the desktop but a non-recessed button for the window does display in the taskbar button area. Whenever you want a minimized window to display and be the active window, click its button in the taskbar button area.

Maximize and Restore Down Buttons

Sometimes when information displays in a window, the information is not completely visible. One method to display the entire contents of a window is to enlarge the window using the **Maximize button**. The Maximize button maximizes a window so the window fills the entire screen, making it easier to see the contents of the window. When a window is maximized, the **Restore Down button** replaces the Maximize button on the title bar. Clicking the Restore Down button will return the window to its size before maximizing. To maximize and restore the My Computer window, complete the following steps.

To Maximize and Restore a Window

1 Point to the Maximize button on the title bar of the My Computer window.

The mouse pointer points to the Maximize button on the My Computer window title bar (Figure 1-18). A ToolTip displays below the Maximize button.

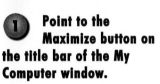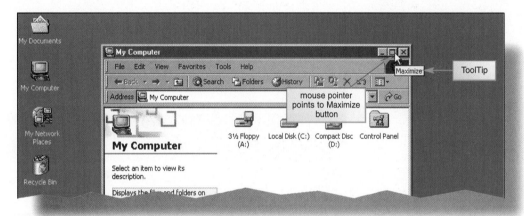

FIGURE 1-18

2 Click the Maximize button.

The My Computer window expands so it and the taskbar fill the desktop (Figure 1-19). The Restore Down button replaces the Maximize button, the My Computer button in the taskbar button area does not change, and the My Computer window still is the active window.

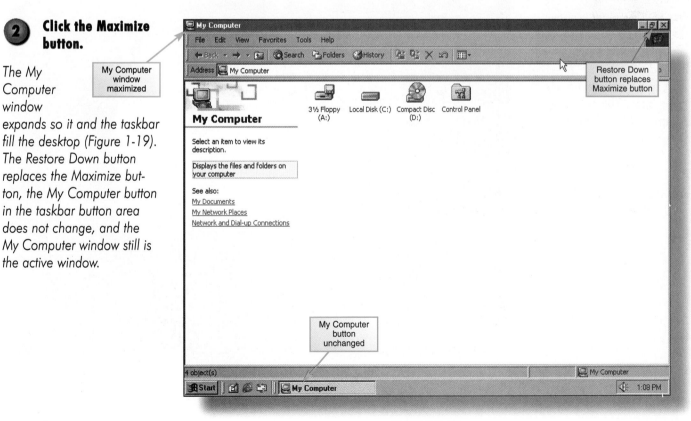

FIGURE 1-19

More About

The Restore Down Button

Hey – this is new in Windows 2000. The button on the title bar that restores the size of a window, which has always been referred to as the Restore button in previous versions of Windows, is now called the Restore Down button. Probably because when you click that button, the window is restored down to a smaller size.

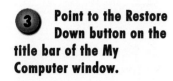

3 **Point to the Restore Down button on the title bar of the My Computer window.**

The mouse pointer points to the Restore Down button on the My Computer window title bar (Figure 1-20). A ToolTip displays below the Restore Down button.

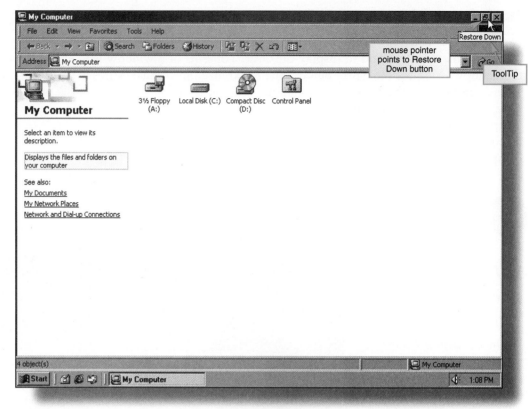

FIGURE 1-20

4 **Click the Restore Down button.**

The My Computer window returns to the size and position it occupied before being maximized (Figure 1-21). The My Computer button does not change. The Maximize button replaces the Restore Down button.

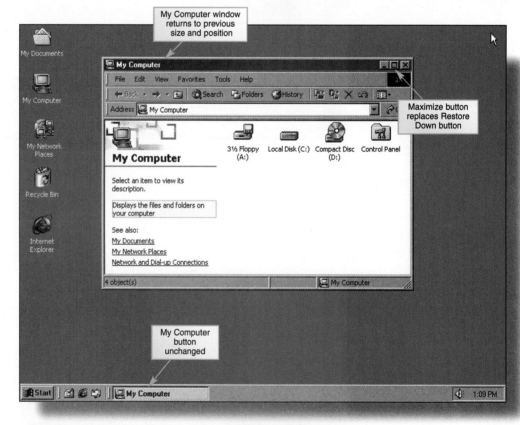

FIGURE 1-21

When a window is maximized, such as in Figure 1-19 on page WIN 1.21, you also can minimize the window by clicking the Minimize button. If, after minimizing the window, you click its button in the taskbar button area, the window will return to its maximized size.

Close Button

The **Close button** on the title bar of a window closes the window and removes the taskbar button from the taskbar. To close and then reopen the My Computer window, complete the following steps.

 To Close and Reopen a Window

1 **Point to the Close button on the title bar of the My Computer window (Figure 1-22).**

More About

The Close Button

In earlier versions of Windows, you had to double-click a button or click a command to close a window. Now you can click the Close button, right-click the title bar and click Close, double-click the window logo on the title bar, or press ALT+F4. Variety is the spice of life!

FIGURE 1-22

2 **Click the Close button.**

The My Computer window closes and the My Computer button no longer displays in the taskbar button area (Figure 1-23).

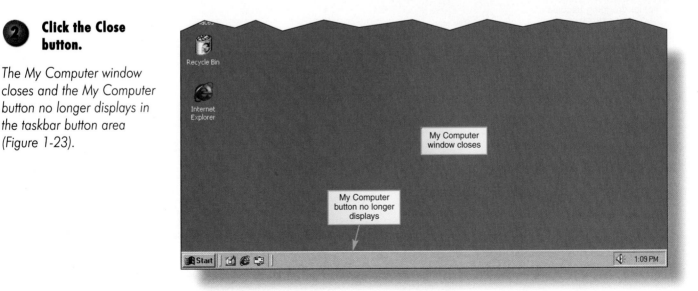

FIGURE 1-23

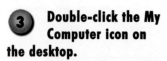

3 **Double-click the My Computer icon on the desktop.**

The My Computer window opens and displays on the desktop (Figure 1-24). The My Computer button displays in the taskbar button area.

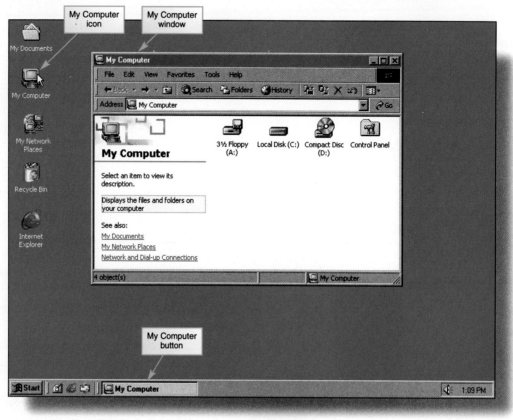

FIGURE 1-24

More About 2000

Dragging

Dragging is the second-most difficult skill to learn with a mouse. You may want to practice dragging a few times so you are comfortable with it. Do not let dragging become a drag – PRACTICE!!

Drag

Drag means you point to an item, hold down the left mouse button, move the item to the desired location, and then release the left mouse button. You can move any open window to another location on the desktop by pointing to the title bar of the window and then dragging the window. To drag the My Computer window to another location on the desktop, perform the following steps.

To Move an Object by Dragging

1 Point to the My Computer window title bar (Figure 1-25).

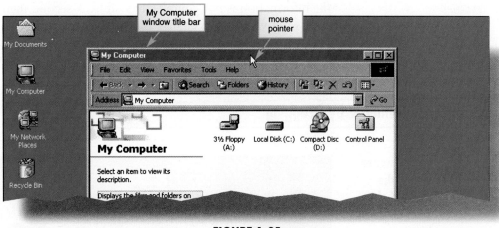

FIGURE 1-25

2 Hold down the left mouse button, move the mouse down so the window moves to the center of the desktop, and then release the left mouse button.

As you drag the My Computer window, the window moves across the desktop. When you release the left mouse button, the window displays in its new location on the desktop (Figure 1-26).

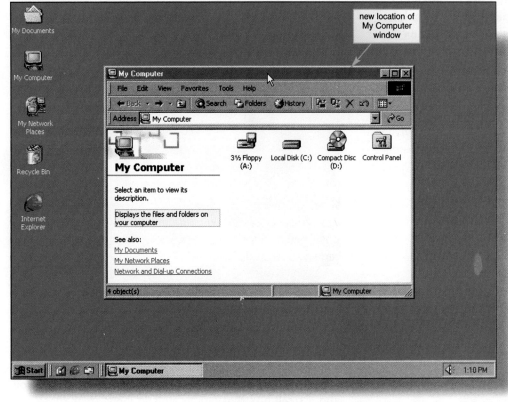

FIGURE 1-26

Sizing a Window by Dragging

As previously mentioned, sometimes when information displays in a window, the information is not completely visible. A second method of displaying information that is not visible is to change the size of the window by dragging the window. For example, you can drag the border of a window to change the size of the window. To change the size of the My Computer window, perform the following step.

Steps To Size a Window by Dragging

1 Position the mouse pointer over the lower-right corner of the My Computer window until the mouse pointer changes to a two-headed arrow. Drag the lower-right corner upward and to the left until the window on the desktop resembles the window shown in Figure 1-27.

As you drag the lower-right corner, the window changes size, the icons in the right panel display in two rows, a vertical scroll bar displays in the left panel, and a portion of the text in the left panel is not visible (Figure 1-27).

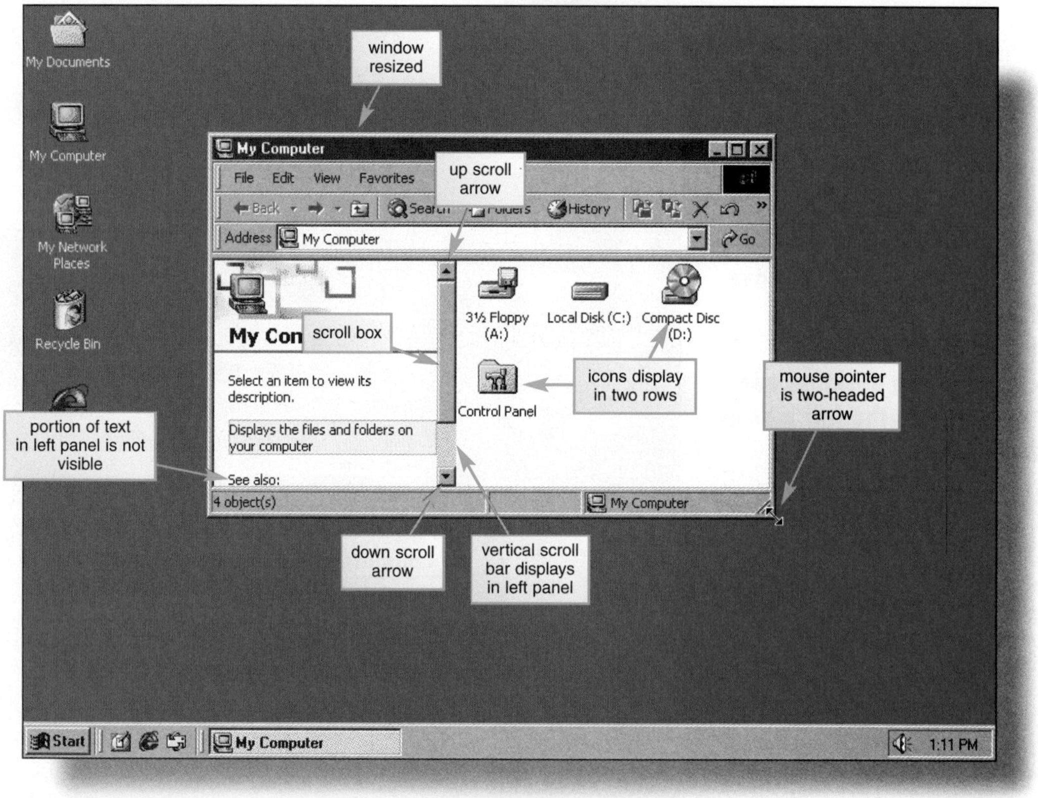

FIGURE 1-27

Window Sizing

Windows 2000 remembers the size of the window when you close the window. When you reopen the window, it will display in the same size as when you closed it.

A **scroll bar** is a bar that displays when the contents of a window are not completely visible. A vertical scroll bar contains an **up scroll arrow**, a **down scroll arrow**, and a **scroll box** that enable you to view areas that currently are not visible. A vertical scroll bar displays along the right edge of the left panel of the My Computer window shown in Figure 1-27. In some cases, the vertical scroll bar also may display along the right edge of the right panel of a window.

In addition to dragging a corner of a window, you also can drag any of the borders of a window. If you drag a vertical border, such as the right border, you can move the border left or right. If you drag a horizontal border, such as the bottom border, you can move the border of the window up or down.

Scrolling in a Window

Previously, two methods were shown to display information that was not completely visible in the My Computer window. These methods were maximizing the My Computer window and changing the size of the My Computer window. The third method uses the scroll bar.

Scrolling can be accomplished in three ways: (1) click the scroll arrows; (2) click the scroll bar; and (3) drag the scroll box. On the following pages, you will use the scroll bar to scroll the contents of the left panel of the My Computer window. Perform the following steps to scroll the left panel of the My Computer window using the scroll arrows.

More About

Scrolling

Most people will either maximize a window or size it so all the objects in the window are visible to avoid scrolling because scrolling takes time. It is more efficient not to have to scroll in a window.

Steps · To Scroll Using Scroll Arrows

1 **Point to the down scroll arrow on the vertical scroll bar (Figure 1-28).**

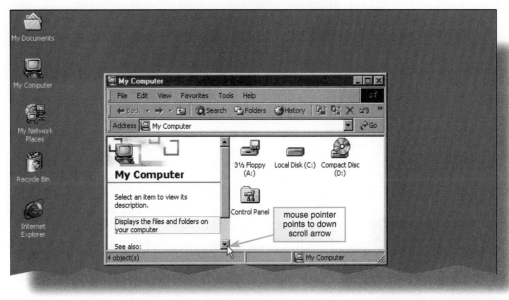

FIGURE 1-28

2 **Click the down scroll arrow one time.**

The left panel scrolls down (the contents in the left panel move up) and displays text at the bottom of the left panel that previously was not visible (Figure 1-29). Because the size of the left panel does not change when you scroll, the contents in the left panel will change, as seen in the difference between Figures 1-28 and 1-29.

FIGURE 1-29

Click the down scroll arrow two more times.

The scroll box moves to the bottom of the scroll bar and the remaining text in the left panel displays (Figure 1-30).

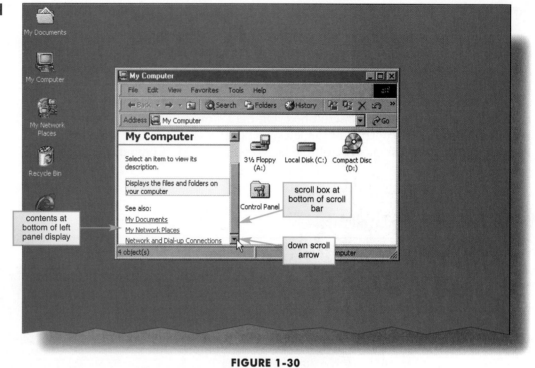

FIGURE 1-30

You can scroll continuously using scroll arrows by pointing to the up or down scroll arrow and holding down the left mouse button. The area being scrolled continues to scroll until you release the left mouse button or you reach the top or bottom of the area. You can also scroll by clicking the scroll bar itself. When you click the scroll bar, the area being scrolled moves up or down a greater distance than when you click the scroll arrows.

The third way in which you can scroll is by dragging the scroll box. When you drag the scroll box, the area being scrolled moves up or down as you drag.

Being able to view the contents of a panel or window by scrolling is an important Windows 2000 skill because in many cases the entire contents of a panel or window are not visible.

Resizing a Window

After moving and resizing a window, you may wish to return the window to approximately its original size. To return the My Computer window to about its original size, complete the following steps.

TO RESIZE A WINDOW

1. Position the mouse pointer over the lower-right corner of the My Computer window border until the mouse pointer changes to a two-headed arrow.

2. Drag the lower-right corner of the My Computer window down and to the right until the window is the same size as shown in Figure 1-26 on page WIN 1.25 and then release the mouse button.

The My Computer window is approximately the same size as it was before you made it smaller.

 **The Scroll Bar**

In many application programs, clicking the scroll bar will move the window a full screen's worth of information up or down. You can step through a word processing document screen by screen, for example, by clicking the scroll bar.

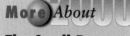 **The Scroll Box**

Dragging the scroll box is the most efficient technique to scroll long distances. In many application programs, such as Microsoft Word, as you scroll using the scroll box, the page number of the document displays next to the scroll box.

Closing a Window

After completing your work in a window, normally you will close the window. To close the My Computer window, complete the following steps.

TO CLOSE A WINDOW

1 Point to the Close button on the right of the title bar in the My Computer window.

2 Click the Close button.

The My Computer window closes and the desktop contains no open windows.

Right-Drag

Right-drag means you point to an item, hold down the right mouse button, move the item to the desired location, and then release the right mouse button. When you right-drag an object, a shortcut menu displays. The shortcut menu contains commands specifically for use with the object being dragged. To right-drag the Launch Outlook Express icon on the Quick Launch toolbar below the icons to the desktop, perform the following steps. If the Launch Outlook Express icon does not display on the Quick Launch toolbar, you will be unable to perform Steps 1 through 3 that follow.

More About

Scrolling Guidelines

General scrolling guidelines: (1) To scroll short distances (line by line), click the scroll arrows; (2) To scroll one screen at a time, click the scroll bar; and (3) To scroll long distances, drag the scroll box.

More About

Right-Dragging

Right-dragging was not available on some earlier versions of Windows, so you might find people familiar with Windows not even considering right-dragging. Because it always produces a shortcut menu, however, right-dragging is the safest way to drag.

Steps) **To Right-Drag**

1 **Point to the Launch Outlook Express icon on the Quick Launch toolbar, hold down the right mouse button, drag the icon below the other icons on the desktop, and then release the right mouse button.**

The dimmed Launch Outlook Express icon and a shortcut menu display on the desktop (Figure 1-31).

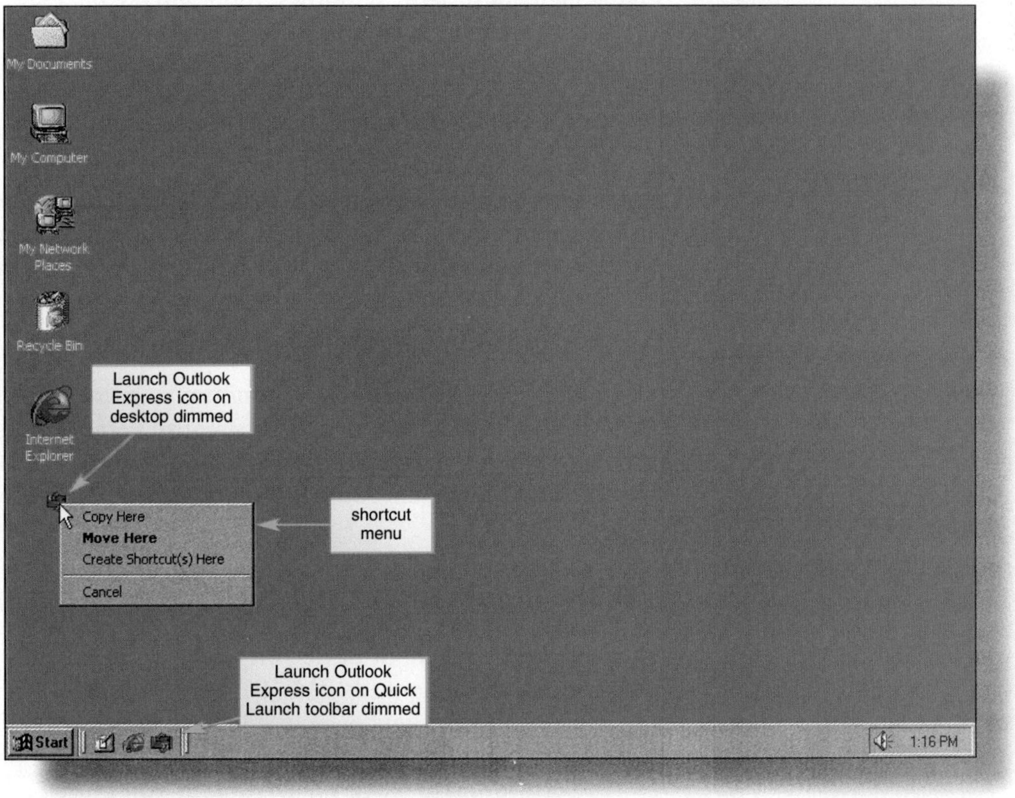

FIGURE 1-31

2 **Point to Cancel on the shortcut menu.**

The Cancel command is highlighted (Figure 1-32).

3 **Click Cancel.**

The shortcut menu and the dragged Launch Outlook Express icon no longer display on the desktop.

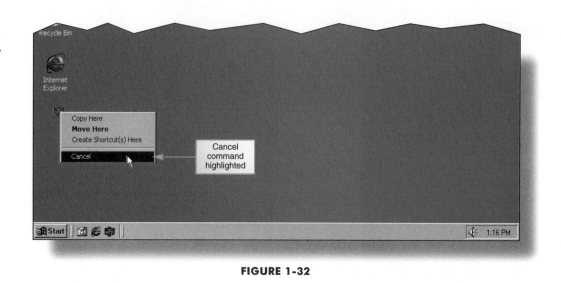

FIGURE 1-32

 More *About*

The Microsoft Keyboard

The Microsoft keyboard in Figure 1-33(b) has special keys for Windows 2000 and is designed ergonomically so you type with your hands apart. It takes a little time to adapt, but several Shelly Cashman Series authors report they type faster, more accurately, and with less fatigue when using the keyboard.

More *About*

Microsoft Keyboards

For additional information about Microsoft keyboards, visit the Microsoft Keyboard Web Site. To visit the site, launch the Internet Explorer browser (see pages WIN 1.32 and 1.35), type www.scsite.com/win2000/more.htm in the Address box and press the ENTER key. To purchase a keyboard, click the buy now button!!!

In Figure 1-31 on the previous page, the original Launch Outlook Express icon remains at its original location on the Quick Launch toolbar and the shortcut menu contains four commands: Copy Here, Move Here, Create Shortcut(s) Here, and Cancel. The Move Here command in bold (dark) font identifies what would happen if you were to drag the Launch Outlook Express icon with the left mouse button.

If you click **Move Here** on the shortcut menu shown, Windows 2000 will move the icon from its current location to the new location. If you click **Copy Here**, Windows 2000 will copy the icon to the new location and two icons will display. Windows 2000 automatically will give the second icon a different name. If you click **Create Shortcut(s) Here**, Windows 2000 will create a special object called a shortcut.

Whenever you begin an operation but do not want to complete the operation, you can click Cancel on a shortcut menu or click the Cancel button in a dialog box. The **Cancel** command will reset anything you have done in the operation.

Although you can move icons by dragging with the primary (left) mouse button and by right-dragging with the secondary (right) mouse button, it is strongly suggested you right-drag because a menu displays and you can specify the exact operation you want to occur. When you drag using the left mouse button, a default operation takes place and the operation may not do what you want.

Summary of Mouse and Windows Operations

You have seen how to use the mouse to point, click, right-click, double-click, drag, and right-drag in order to accomplish certain tasks on the desktop. The use of a mouse is an important skill when using Windows 2000. In addition, you have learned how to move around and use windows on the Windows 2000 desktop.

The Keyboard and Keyboard Shortcuts

The **keyboard** is an input device on which you manually key in, or type, data. Figure 1-33a shows the enhanced IBM 101-key keyboard, and Figure 1-33b shows a Microsoft Natural keyboard designed specifically for use with Windows. Many tasks you accomplish with a mouse also can be accomplished using a keyboard.

To perform tasks using the keyboard, you must understand the notation used to identify which keys to press. This notation is used throughout Windows 2000 to identify a **keyboard shortcut**.

FIGURE 1-33a

FIGURE 1-33b

Keyboard shortcuts consist of: (1) pressing a single key (such as press the ENTER key); or (2) pressing and holding down one key and pressing a second key, as shown by two key names separated by a plus sign (such as press CTRL+ESC). For example, to obtain Help about Windows 2000, you can press the F1 key; to display the Start menu, hold down the CTRL key and then press the ESC key (press CTRL+ESC).

Often, computer users will use keyboard shortcuts for operations they perform frequently. For example, many users find pressing the F1 key to launch Windows 2000 Help easier than using the Start menu as shown later in this project. As a user, you probably will find the combination of keyboard and mouse operations that particularly suit you, but it is strongly recommended that generally you use the mouse.

Launching an Application Program

One of the basic tasks you can perform using Windows 2000 is to launch an application program. A **program** is a set of computer instructions that carries out a task on the computer. An **application program** is a program that allows you to accomplish a specific task for which that program is designed. For example, a **word processing program** is an application program that allows you to create written documents; a **presentation graphics program** is an application program that allows you to create graphic presentations for display on a computer; and a **Web browser program** is an application program that allows you to search for and display Web pages.

The most common activity on a computer is to run an application program to accomplish tasks using the computer. You can launch an application program in a variety of ways. When several methods are available to accomplish a task, a computer user has the opportunity to try various methods and select the method that best fits his or her needs.

To illustrate the variety of methods available to launch an application program, three methods will be shown to launch the Internet Explorer Web browser program. These methods include using the Start button; using the Quick Launch toolbar; and using an icon on the desktop.

The Internet Keyboard

Microsoft's newest keyboard, the Internet keyboard, has keys for accessing the Internet and sending and retrieving e-mail. For a peek at what might be the keyboard of the future, follow the instructions in the More About at the bottom of the previous page and click the Internet Keyboard link.

Application Programs

Several application programs (Internet Explorer, Paint, Notepad, and Pinball) are part of Windows 2000. Most application programs, however, such as Microsoft Word, Microsoft Access, and others must be purchased separately.

Launching an Application Using the Start Button

The first method of launching an application program is to use the Start menu. Perform the following steps to launch Internet Explorer using the Start menu and Internet Explorer command.

Steps) **To Launch a Program Using the Start Menu**

1 **Click the Start button on the taskbar, point to Programs on the Start menu, and then point to Internet Explorer on the Programs submenu.**

*The Start menu and Programs submenu display (Figure 1-34). The Programs submenu contains the **Internet Explorer command** to launch the Internet Explorer program. You might find more, fewer, or different commands on the Start menu and Programs submenu on your computer.*

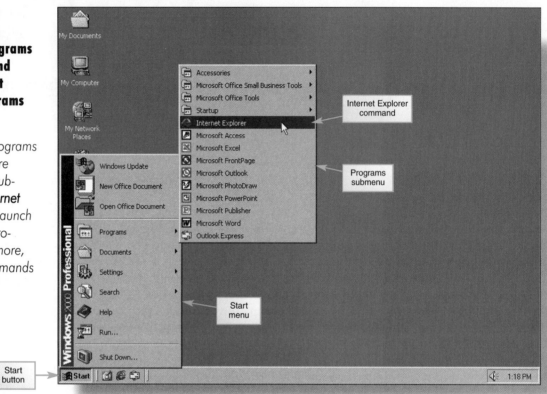

FIGURE 1-34

The Contents sheet in the navigation pane contains 16 entries. The first entry is identified by an open book and document icon, and the highlighted Start Here name. The **open book and document icon** indicates additional information or an overview is available for the entry. The Start Here entry is highlighted to indicate additional information about the entry displays in the topic pane. The topic pane contains the **Start Here screen**. The Start Here screen contains a table of contents consisting of four items (Find it fast, If you've used Windows before, Troubleshooting, and Information and support on the Web).

A closed book icon precedes each of the remaining 15 entries in the Contents sheet. The **closed book icon** indicates that Help topics or more books are contained in a book but do not display in the Contents sheet. Clicking the Index tab, Search tab, or Favorites tab in the navigation pane displays the Index, Search, or Favorites sheet, respectively.

In addition to launching Help by using the Start button, you also can launch Help by clicking an open area of the desktop and pressing the F1 key.

After launching Help, the next step is to find the topic in which you are interested. Assume you want to find information about locating a Help topic. Perform the following steps to find the topic that describes how to find a topic in Help.

To Use the Contents Sheet to Find a Help Topic

1 **Point to the Introducing Windows 2000 Professional closed book icon in the navigation pane.**

The mouse pointer changes to a hand when positioned on the icon and the Introducing Windows 2000 Professional book name displays in blue font and underlined (Figure 1-40).

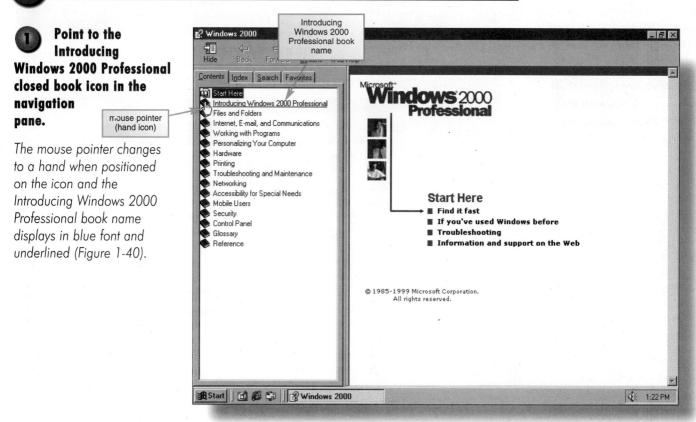

FIGURE 1-40

② Click the Introducing Windows 2000 Professional closed book icon and then point to the How to Use Help closed book icon.

Windows 2000 opens the Introducing Windows 2000 Professional book, changes the closed book icon to an open book icon, highlights the Introducing Windows 2000 Professional book name, underlines the How to Use Help book name, and displays the name and underline in blue font (Figure 1-41). The **open book icon** indicates that Help topics or books contained in the book display indented below the book.

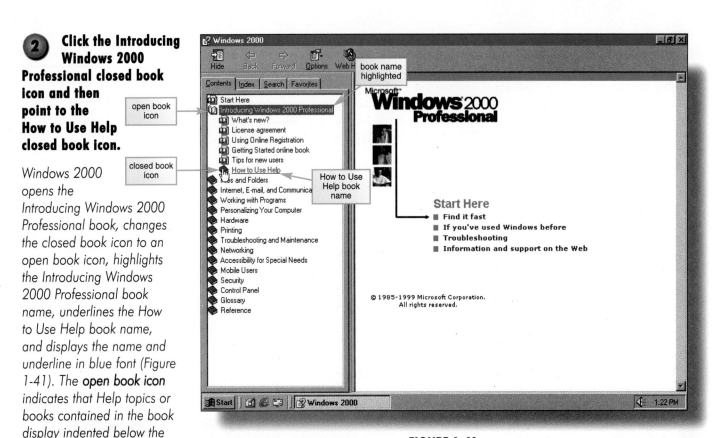

FIGURE 1-41

③ Click the How to Use Help closed book icon and then point to Find a Help topic.

Windows 2000 opens the How to Use Help book, changes the closed book icon to an open book icon, highlights the How to Use Help book name, underlines the Find a Help topic name, and displays the topic name and underline in blue font (Figure 1-42). The **question mark icon** indicates a Help topic without further subdivisions. Clicking the **Help overview icon** displays an overview of the Help system.

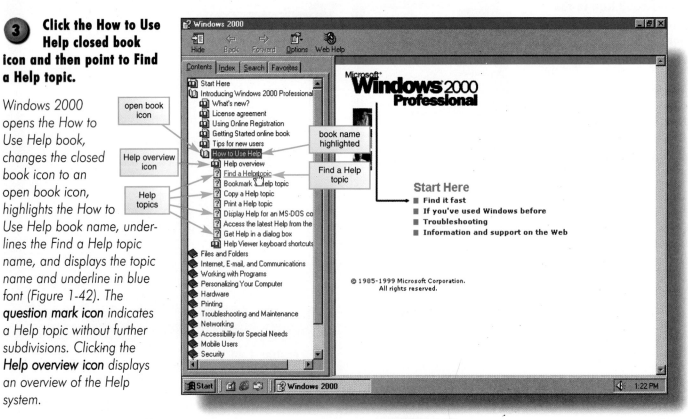

FIGURE 1-42

4 **Click Find a Help topic and then read the information about finding a Help topic in the topic pane.**

*Windows 2000 highlights the Find a Help topic name and displays information about finding a Help topic in the topic pane (Figure 1-43). Clicking the **plus sign** in the small box to the left of the Contents tab, Index tab, Search tab, or Favorites tab entries displays additional information about the entry.*

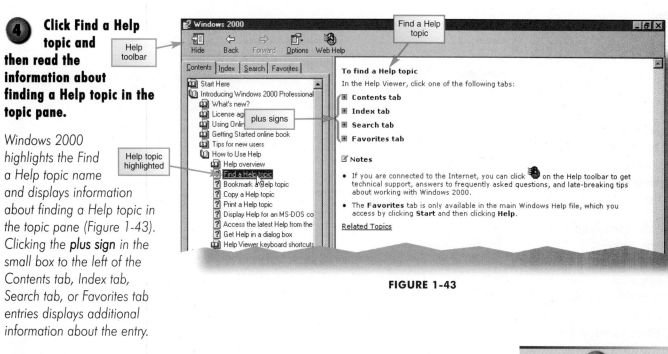

FIGURE 1-43

In Figure 1-43, the Help toolbar contains five icons. If you click the **Hide button** on the Help toolbar, Windows 2000 hides the tabs in the navigation pane and displays only the topic pane in the Windows 2000 window. Clicking the **Back button** or **Forward button** displays a previously displayed Help topic in the topic pane. Clicking the **Options button** allows you to hide or display the tabs in the navigation pane, display previously displayed Help topics in the topic pane, stop the display of a Help topic, refresh the currently displayed Help topic, access the Internet options, access Web Help, and print a Help topic. The **Web Help command** on the Options menu and the **Web Help button** on the Help toolbar allow you to use the Internet to obtain technical support, answers to frequently asked questions, and tips about working with Windows 2000.

Notice also in Figure 1-43 that the Windows 2000 title bar contains a Minimize button, Restore Down button, and Close button. You can minimize or restore the Windows 2000 window as needed and also close the Windows 2000 window.

Index Sheet

A second method of finding answers to your questions about Windows 2000 or application programs running under Windows 2000 is to use the Index sheet. The **Index sheet** contains a list of index entries, each of which references one or more Help screens. Assume you want more information about the desktop and the objects on the desktop. Perform the steps on the next page to learn more about the desktop and the objects on the desktop.

Other Ways

1. Press DOWN ARROW until book name is highlighted, press RIGHT ARROW (or ENTER), continue until Help topic displays, press ENTER, read Help topic

More About

The Index Sheet

The Index sheet probably is the best source of information in Windows Help because you can enter the subject in which you are interested. Sometimes, however, you will have to be creative to discover the index entry that answers your question because the most obvious entry will not always lead to your answer.

Steps To Use the Index Sheet

1 **Click the Index tab, type** desktop **in the Type in the keyword to find text box, and then point to overview in the list.**

The Index sheet, containing the Type in the keyword to find text box, a list box, and Display button, displays (Figure 1-44). When you type an entry in the text box, the list of index entries in the list box automatically scrolls and the entry you type (desktop) is highlighted in the list. Several entries display indented below the desktop entry.

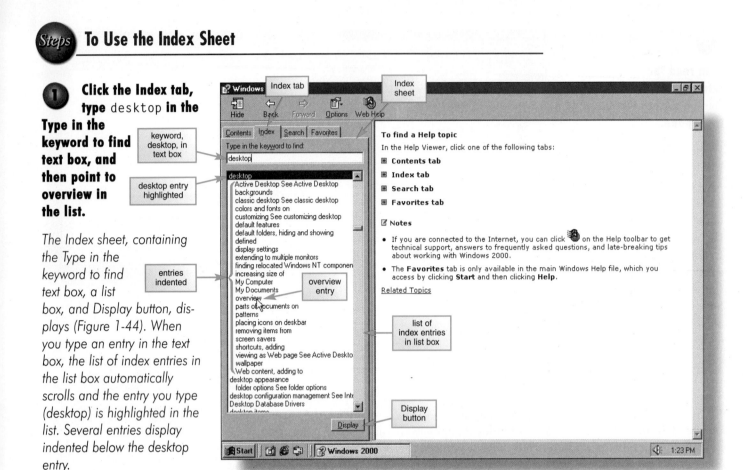

FIGURE 1-44

2 **Click overview and then point to the Display button at the bottom of the Index sheet.**

Windows 2000 displays the desktop, overview entry in the text box and highlights the overview entry in the list (Figure 1-45).

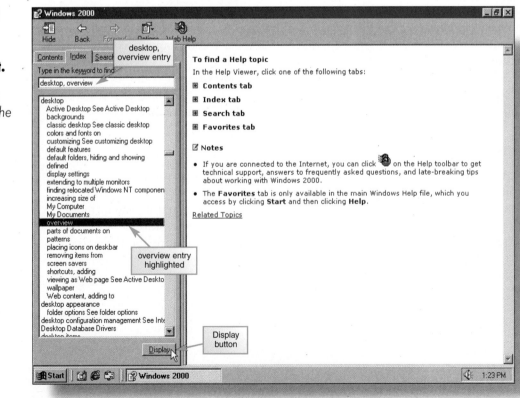

FIGURE 1-45

Click the Display button.

The Desktop overview topic displays in the topic pane (Figure 1-46). The topic contains an overview of the desktop, a list of desktop features, and several links (shortcuts, programs, active content, channel, Windows 2000 Professional Getting Started, and Related Topics). Clicking the plus sign in the small box to the left of a desktop feature displays additional information about that feature.

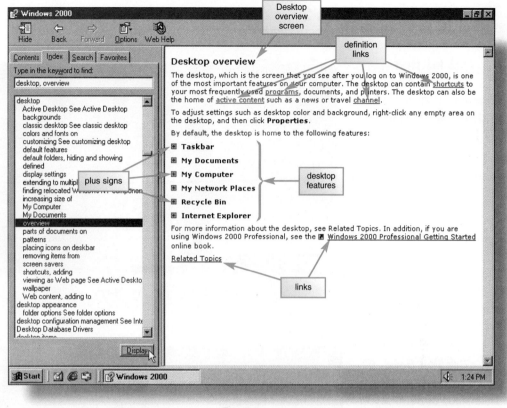

FIGURE 1-46

Other Ways

1. Press ALT+N, type keyword, press DOWN ARROW until topic is highlighted, press ALT+D (or ENTER)

In Figure 1-46, the shortcuts, programs, active content, and channel links are underlined and display in green font to indicate that clicking a link will display its definition. Clicking anywhere off the definition removes the definition.

The Windows 2000 Professional Getting Started and Related Topics links are underlined and display in blue font. Clicking the Windows 2000 Professional Getting Started link displays the Getting Started online book that helps you install Windows 2000, use the desktop, learn about new features, connect to a network, and find answers to commonly asked questions. Clicking the Related Topics link displays a pop-up window that contains topics related to the desktop overview topic.

After using Windows Help, normally you will close Windows Help. To close Windows Help, complete the following step.

TO CLOSE WINDOWS HELP

1 Click the Close button on the title bar of the Windows 2000 window.

Windows 2000 closes the Windows 2000 window.

Shutting Down Windows 2000

After completing your work with Windows 2000, you may want to shut down Windows 2000 using the **Shut Down command** on the Start menu. If you are sure you want to shut down Windows 2000, perform the following steps. If you are not sure about shutting down Windows 2000, read the steps on the next page without actually performing them.

More About

Shut Down Procedures

Some users of Windows 2000 have turned off their computers without following the shut down procedure only to find data they thought they had stored on disk was lost. Because of the way Windows 2000 writes data on the disk, it is important you shut down Windows properly so you do not lose your work.

Steps To Shut Down Windows 2000

1 **Click the Start button on the taskbar and then point to Shut Down on the Start menu (Figure 1-47).**

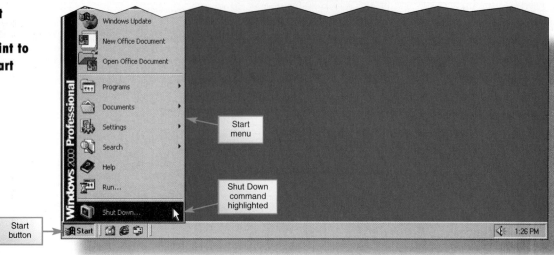

FIGURE 1-47

2 **Click Shut Down. If necessary, use the UP ARROW key or DOWN ARROW key to display the words, Shut down, in the What do you want the computer to do? box. Point to the OK button.**

The desktop darkens and the Shut Down Windows dialog box displays (Figure 1-48). The dialog box contains the What do you want the computer to do? box and three command buttons. The highlighted command, Shut down, displays in the box.

3 **Click the OK button.**

Windows 2000 is shut down.

FIGURE 1-48

Other Ways

1. Press CTRL+ESC, press U, use ARROW keys to select Shut down, press ENTER

2. Press ALT+F4, use ARROW keys to select Shut down, press ENTER

While Windows 2000 is shutting down, two dialog boxes display momentarily on a blue background. First, the Please Wait dialog box containing the Windows 2000 logo, Windows 2000 name, and the text, saving your settings, displays momentarily. Then, the Shutdown in Progress dialog box, containing the text, Please wait while the system writes unsaved data to disk, displays. At this point you can turn off the computer. When shutting down Windows 2000, you should never turn off the computer before these two dialog boxes display.

If you accidentally click Shut Down on the Start menu and you do not want to shut down Windows 2000, click the Cancel button in the Shut Down Windows dialog box to return to normal Windows 2000 operation.

CASE PERSPECTIVE SUMMARY

While continuing to answer questions about Windows 2000 Professional in the workplace, you spent nearly every free moment in the next two weeks learning about the newly installed operating system. Then, the daily training sessions kept you busy for the following three months. You taught 35 workshops and trained all of the 462 employees in the company. Your supervisor, who attended the Windows 2000 Professional seminar, complimented your success by giving you a sizable pay raise and time off to attend the annual Comdex computer convention in Las Vegas, Nevada.

Project Summary

Project 1 illustrated the Microsoft Windows 2000 graphical user interface. You launched Windows 2000, learned the parts of the desktop, and learned to point, click, right-click, double-click, drag, and right-drag. You opened, minimized, maximized, restored, and closed a Windows 2000 window, as well as learning several methods of launching an application. Using the Contents and Index sheet, you obtained Help about Microsoft Windows 2000. You shut down Windows 2000 using the Shut Down command on the Start menu.

What You Should Know

Having completed this project, you now should be able to perform the following tasks:

- Close a Window *(WIN 1.29)*
- Close and Reopen a Window *(WIN 1.23)*
- Close the Getting Started with Windows 2000 Window *(WIN 1.12)*
- Close Windows Help *(WIN 1.41)*
- Launch a Program Using an Icon on the Desktop *(WIN 1.35)*
- Launch a Program Using the Quick Launch Toolbar *(WIN 1.34)*
- Launch a Program Using the Start Menu *(WIN 1.32)*
- Launch Windows Help *(WIN 1.36)*
- Maximize and Restore a Window *(WIN 1.21)*

- Minimize and Redisplay a Window *(WIN 1.19)*
- Move an Object by Dragging *(WIN 1.25)*
- Open a Window by Double-Clicking *(WIN 1.17)*
- Point and Click *(WIN 1.14)*
- Resize a Window *(WIN 1.28)*
- Right-Click *(WIN 1.16)*
- Right-Drag *(WIN 1.29)*
- Scroll Using Scroll Arrows *(WIN 1.27)*
- Shut Down Windows 2000 *(WIN 1.42)*
- Size a Window by Dragging *(WIN 1.26)*
- Use the Contents Sheet to Find a Help Topic *(WIN 1.37)*
- Use the Index Sheet *(WIN 1.40)*

Test Your Knowledge

1 True/False

Instructions: Circle T if the statement is true or F if the statement is false.

T   F   1. A user interface is a combination of computer hardware and computer software.

T   F   2. The Quick Launch toolbar displays on the taskbar at the bottom of the desktop.

T   F   3. Click means press the right mouse button.

T   F   4. When you drag an object onto the desktop, Windows 2000 displays a shortcut menu.

T   F   5. Double-clicking the My Computer icon on the desktop opens a window.

T   F   6. You can maximize a window by dragging the title bar of the window.

T   F   7. One of the basic tasks you can perform using Windows 2000 is to launch an application program.

T   F   8. You can launch Windows Help by clicking the Start button and then clicking Help on the Start menu.

T   F   9. To find an entry in the Index sheet, type the first few characters of the entry in the text box in the Contents sheet.

T   F   10. You click the Close button to shut down Windows 2000.

2 Multiple Choice

Instructions: Circle the correct response.

1. Through a user interface, the user is able to _____ .
   a. control the computer
   b. request information from the computer
   c. respond to messages displayed by the computer
   d. all of the above

2. A shortcut menu displays when you _____ a(n) _____ .
   a. right-click, object
   b. click, menu name on the menu bar
   c. click, submenu
   d. click, recessed button in the taskbar button area

3. In this book, a dark blue title bar and a recessed button in the taskbar button area indicate a window is _____ .
   a. inactive
   b. minimized
   c. closed
   d. active

4. Text that is underlined and displays in blue font is a(n) _____ .
   a. uniform resource locator
   b. hyperlink
   c. hypertext document
   d. definition

Test Your Knowledge

5. To view the contents of a window that are not currently visible in the window, use the _____ .
   a. title bar
   b. scroll bar
   c. menu bar
   d. Restore Down button

6. _____ is holding down the right mouse button, moving an item to the desired location, and then releasing the right mouse button.
   a. Double-clicking
   b. Right-clicking
   c. Right-dragging
   d. Pointing

7. Which method cannot be used to launch the Internet Explorer application?
   a. Click the Start button, point to Programs, and then click Internet Explorer.
   b. Click the Launch Internet Explorer Browser icon on the Quick Launch toolbar.
   c. Click the Internet Explorer button on the Standard Buttons toolbar.
   d. Click the Internet Explorer icon on the desktop.

8. To browse through Help topics by category, use the _____ sheet.
   a. Index
   b. Contents
   c. Search
   d. Favorites

9. For information about an index entry in the Index sheet, click the index entry and _____ .
   a. press the F1 key
   b. click the Forward button on the toolbar
   c. click the Search tab
   d. click the Display button

10. To shut down Windows 2000, _____ .
   a. click the Start button, select Shut Down, and then click the OK button
   b. click File on the menu bar and then click Shut Down
   c. right-click the taskbar, click Shut Down on the shortcut menu, and then click the OK button
   d. press the F10 key and then click the OK button

3 Identifying the Objects on the Desktop

Instructions: On the desktop shown in Figure 1-49 on the next page, arrows point to several items or objects on the desktop. Identify the items or objects in the spaces provided.

(continued)

Test Your Knowledge

Identifying the Objects on the Desktop *(continued)*

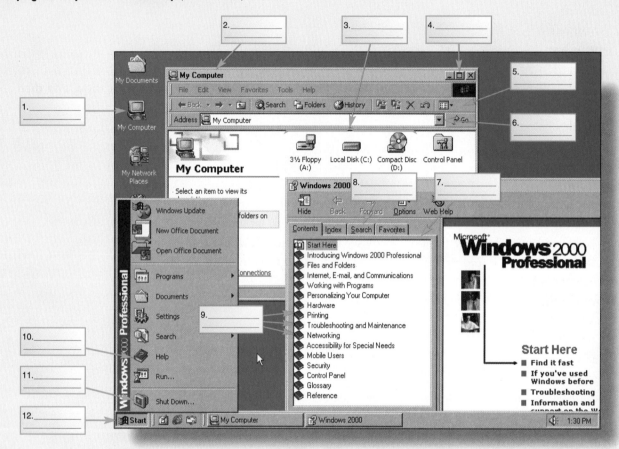

FIGURE 1-49

4 Launching the Internet Explorer Browser

Instructions: In the spaces provided, list the steps for the three methods of launching the Internet Explorer browser used in this project.

Method 1:

Step 1: _____

Step 2: _____

Step 3: _____

Step 4: _____

Method 2:

Step 1: _____

Method 3:

Step 1: _____

Use Help

1 Using Windows Help

Instructions: Use Windows Help and a computer to perform the following tasks.

Part 1: *Using the Question Mark Button*

1. If necessary, start Microsoft Windows 2000.
2. Right-click an open area of the desktop to display a shortcut menu.
3. Click Properties on the shortcut menu to display the Display Properties dialog box.
4. Click the Background tab in the Display Properties dialog box.
5. Click the Question Mark button on the title bar. The mouse pointer changes to a block arrow with a question mark.
6. Click the list box in the Background sheet. A pop-up window displays explaining the list box. Read the information in the pop-up window and summarize the function of the list box. _____

   _____
7. Click an open area of the Background sheet to remove the pop-up window.
8. Click the question mark button on the title bar and then click the Pattern button. A pop-up window displays explaining what happens when you click this button. Read the information in the pop-up window and summarize the function of the button. _____

   _____
9. Click an open area in the Background sheet to remove the pop-up window.
10. Click the question mark button on the title bar and then click the monitor icon in the Background sheet. A pop-up window displays explaining the function of the monitor. Read the information in the pop-up window and summarize the function of the monitor. _____

    _____
11. Click an open area in the Background sheet to remove the pop-up window.
12. Click the question mark button on the title bar and then click the Cancel button. A pop-up window displays explaining what happens when you click the button. Read the information in the pop-up window and summarize the function of the Cancel button. _____

    _____
13. Click an open area in the Background sheet to remove the pop-up window.
14. Click the Cancel button in the Display Properties dialog box.

Part 2: *Finding What's New in Windows 2000*

1. Click the Start button and then click Help on the Start menu.
2. Click the Maximize button on Windows 2000 title bar.
3. If the Contents sheet does not display, click the Contents tab in the navigation pane. Click the Introducing Windows 2000 Professional closed book icon.
4. Click the What's new? icon in the Contents sheet and then click the plus sign in a small box preceding the More powerful entry in the topic pane. The three ways that Windows 2000 Professional makes using a computer more powerful display in the topic pane.
5. Click the Options button on the Help toolbar to display the Options menu and then click Print.

(continued)

Use Help

Using Windows Help *(continued)*

6. Click the OK button in the Print Topics dialog box. Click the Print button in the Print dialog box to print the What's new topic.
7. Click the Related Topics link in the topic pane to display a pop-up window containing three related topics. List the three topics. _____
8. Click the Reliability topic in the pop-up window.
9. Click the Options button on the Help toolbar to display the Options menu and then click Print.
10. Click the OK button in the Print Topics dialog box. Click the Print button in the Print dialog box to print the What's new topic screen.

Part 3: *Viewing Tips for New Windows 2000 Users*

1. Click the Tips for new users icon in the Contents sheet. The Tips for new users screen displays in the topic pane.
2. Click the plus sign in the small box preceding the Change the appearance of items in a folder entry in the topic pane and then click the Step-by-step procedure link. The steps to follow to change the appearance of the items in a folder display. What is the first step in the procedure?_____
3. Click the Back button on the Help toolbar to display the Tips for new users screen.
4. Click the plus sign in the small box preceding the Add Web content to your desktop entry in the topic pane. What types of content can you add to the desktop?_____
   _____
5. Click the Step-by-step procedure link. What are the three instructions to follow to add content to the desktop?_____
   _____
   _____

Part 4: *Reading About the Getting Started Online Book*

1. Click the Getting Started online book icon in the navigation pane. Read the information Windows 2000 displays about the *Getting Started online book* in the topic pane. The *Getting Started online book* is the printed manual for Windows 2000.
2. Click the Windows 2000 Professional Getting Started link in the topic pane to display the Windows 2000 Professional Getting Started window.
3. If the Contents sheet does not display, click the Contents tab. Click the Preface closed book icon. Click and read the three Help topics.
4. Click the open book icon (followed by a right arrow) in the upper-right corner of the topic pane until you have displayed and read each topic in the Ch.1 - Welcome book.
5. Click the open book icon (preceded by a left arrow) in the upper-left corner of the topic pane to display previously displayed topics.
6. Read the remaining chapters and appendices in the *Getting Started online book*.
7. Click the Close button in the Windows 2000 Professional Getting Started window.
8. Click the Close button in the Windows 2000 window.

Use Help

2 Using Windows Help to Obtain Help

Instructions: Use Windows Help and a computer to perform the following tasks.

1. Find Help about keyboard shortcuts by looking in the Reference book in the Contents sheet. Answer the following questions in the spaces provided.
   a. What Windows 2000 keyboard shortcut is used to view properties for a selected item?
   _____
   b. What Windows 2000 keyboard shortcut is used to display the shortcut menu for a selected item?
   _____
   c. What Help Viewer keyboard shortcut is used to display the Options menu?
   _____
   d. What Help Viewer keyboard shortcut is used to display the Index tab?_____
   e. What Natural Keyboard shortcut is used to display or hide the Start menu? _____
   f. What Natural Keyboard shortcut is used to open My Computer? _____
2. Use the Index sheet to answer the following questions in the spaces provided.
   a. How do you get Help in a dialog box?_____
   _____
   b. What dialog box do you use to change the appearance of the mouse pointer?_____
   _____
   c. How do you minimize all windows? _____
   _____
   d. What is a server? _____
   _____
3. Find Help about viewing the Start Here screen (also called the **Welcome screen**) that displays when you launch Windows 2000. Use the search word, welcome, and the Search sheet. The Viewing the Welcome screen should display. Answer the following questions in the spaces provided.
   a. How can you open the Welcome screen from the Viewing the Welcome screen? _____
   _____
   b. How can you open the Welcome screen using the Start menu? _____
   _____
   c. Open the Welcome screen. How many entries display in the Table of Contents in the Getting Started screen? _____
   d. Point to Discover Windows 2000 in the table of contents. What does the Discover Windows 2000 Professional tour highlight? _____
   _____
   e. Close the Getting Started with Windows 2000 window.
4. Find Help about what to do if you have a problem in Windows 2000. The tools to solve a problem while using Windows 2000 are called troubleshooters. Using Help, locate the Troubleshooters overview. Answer the following questions in the spaces provided.
   a. What does a troubleshooter allow you to diagnose and solve? _____
   _____

(continued)

Use Help

Using Windows Help to Obtain Help *(continued)*

    b. List five of the Windows 2000 troubleshooters. _____

_____

5. Obtain information on software licensing by answering the following questions. Find and then print information from Windows Help that supports your answers.

    a. How does the law protect computer software? _____

_____

    b. What is software piracy? _____

_____

    c. Why should I be concerned about it? _____

_____

    d. What is an EULA (end user licensing agreement)?

_____

    e. Can you make a second copy of an operating system (Windows 2000) for use at home, work, or on a portable computer? _____

    f. How can you identify illegal Microsoft software? _____

_____

6. Find the definition for the following terms using the Glossary book in the Contents sheet. Write the definitions in the spaces provided.

    a. desktop pattern _____

    b. My Documents _____

    c. screen saver _____

    d. server _____

    e. virus _____

7. Use the Reference book in the Contents sheet to view the Programs list. Answer the following questions in the spaces provided.

    a. What is the purpose of the Address Book? _____

_____

    b. For what purpose would you use a certificate? _____

_____

    c. What information does Device Manager provide? _____

_____

    d. What does Outlook Express allow you to do? _____

    e. What is Paint? _____

8. Close all open windows.

In the Lab

1 Improving Your Mouse Skills

Instructions: Use a computer to perform the following tasks.

1. If necessary, start Microsoft Windows 2000.
2. Click the Start button on the taskbar, point to Programs on the Start menu, point to Accessories on the Programs submenu, point to Games on the Accessories submenu, and click Solitaire on the Games submenu.
3. Click the Maximize button in the Solitaire window.
4. Click Help on the Solitaire menu bar and then click Contents. If the Contents sheet does not display, click the Contents tab.
5. Read the Solitaire overview and the three Help topics (Play Solitaire, Change game options, and Choose a scoring system) in the Solitaire book.
6. After reviewing the Help topics, close the Solitaire window.
7. Play the game of Solitaire.
8. Click the Close button on the Solitaire title bar to close the game.

2 Using the Discover Windows 2000 Professional Tour

Instructions: To use the Discover Windows 2000 Professional tour you will need a copy of the Windows 2000 Professional CD-ROM. If this CD-ROM is not available, skip this lab assignment. Otherwise, use a computer and the CD-ROM to perform the following tasks.

Part 1: *Launching the Discover Windows 2000 Professional Tour*
1. If necessary, start Microsoft Windows 2000.
2. Insert the Windows 2000 Professional CD-ROM in the CD-ROM drive. If the Microsoft Windows 2000 CD window displays, click the Close button in the window to close the window.
3. Click the Start button on the taskbar, click Run on the Start menu, type welcome in the Open box in the Run dialog box, and click the OK button. The Getting Started with Windows 2000 window, containing a table of contents, displays.
4. Click Discover Windows in the table of contents. The Discover screen displays. The right panel contains four categories (Easier to Use, Easier to Manage, More Compatible, and More Powerful), and the left panel contains instructions for selecting a category in the right panel.

Part 2: *Starting the Tour*
1. Click Easier to Use in the right panel. A toolbar containing the four categories displays, the five topics in the Easier to Use category display in the left panel, and the right panel contains information about the Easier to Use category. Read the information.

(continued)

In the Lab

Using the Discover Windows 2000 Professional Tour *(continued)*

Part 3: *Touring the Easier to Use Category*

1. Click Work with Files in the left panel. Four subtopics display indented below the Work with Files topic in the left panel and the right panel contains information about the Work with Files topic. Read the information.

2. Click Track Your Documents. Four subtopics display indented below the Track Your Documents subtopic in the left panel, and the right panel contains information about the Track Your Documents subtopic. Read the information.

3. Click My Network Places. Information about the My Network Places subtopic displays in right panel. Read the information.

4. Click each of the remaining subtopics (My Documents, File Open/Save As, and History Folder) in the Track Your Documents subtopic. When a Play Animation button displays, click the button to view an animated explanation of the subtopic. Answer the following question.
   a. In what folder does Windows 2000 Professional save all documents? _____
   _____

5. Click the remaining subtopics in the Track Your Documents topic (Associate File Types, Work with Images, and Manage Your Printing) in the Work with Files topic.

6. Tour the remaining topics (Find Information, Personalize, Work on the Web, and Work Remotely) in the Easier to Use category. Answer the following questions.
   a. Which dialog box do you use to search the disk drive, network, or Internet?_____
   _____
   b. Which wizard do you use to establish a new Internet user account?_____
   _____
   c. If you lose your portable computer, what prevents others from viewing the files on the computer?
   _____

Part 4: *Touring the Other Categories*

1. Tour the other three categories (Easier to Manage, More Compatible, and More Powerful) and answer the following questions.
   a. The ability to upgrade from Windows 95 and Windows 98 to Windows 2000 is based on what requirement?_____
   b. What is the comprehensive list of devices supported by Windows 2000 called? _____
   _____
   c. What is IEEE 1394? _____
   _____
   d. What is a self-healing program? _____
   e. Disk space storage is more efficient because of what storage system?_____
   _____

2. Click Exit in the left panel to quit the tour.

3. Click the Close button in the Getting Started with Windows 2000 window.

4. Remove the Windows 2000 CD-ROM from the CD-ROM drive.

In the Lab

3 Launching and Using the Internet Explorer Application

Instructions: Perform the following steps to launch the Internet Explorer application.

Part 1: *Launching the Internet Explorer Application*

1. Start Microsoft Windows 2000 and, if necessary, connect to the Internet.
2. Click the Launch Internet Explorer Browser icon on the Quick Launch toolbar. Maximize the Microsoft Internet Explorer window.
3. If the Address bar does not display below the Standard Buttons toolbar in the Microsoft Internet Explorer window, click View on the menu bar, point to Toolbars, and click Address bar on the Toolbars submenu.

Part 2: *Entering a URL in the Address Bar*

1. Click the URL in the Address bar to highlight the URL.
2. Type www.microsoft.com in the Address bar and then press the ENTER key.
3. Answer the following questions.
   a. What URL displays in the Address bar? _____
   b. What window title displays on the title bar? _____
4. If necessary, scroll the Web page to view the contents of the Web page. List five hyperlinks (underlined text) that are shown on this Web page. _____
   _____
5. Click any hyperlink on the Web page. What hyperlink did you click? _____
   _____
6. Describe the Web page that displayed when you clicked the hyperlink? _____
   _____
7. Click the Print button on the Standard Buttons toolbar to print the Web page.

Part 3: *Entering a URL in the Address Bar*

1. Click the URL in the Address bar to highlight the URL.
2. Type www.disney.com in the Address bar and then press the ENTER key.
3. What window title displays on the title bar? _____
4. Scroll the Web page to view the contents of the Web page. Do any graphic images display on the Web page?
   _____
   If so, describe two images. _____
5. Pointing to an image on a Web page and having the mouse pointer change to a hand indicates the image is a hyperlink. Does the Web page include an image that is a hyperlink? _____
   If so, describe the image. _____
6. Click the hyperlink to display another Web page. What window title displays on the title bar?
   _____
7. Click the Print button on the Standard Buttons toolbar to print the Web page.

(continued)

In the Lab

Launching and Using the Internet Explorer Application *(continued)*

Part 4: *Displaying Previously Displayed Web Pages*

1. Click the Back button on the Standard Buttons toolbar. What Web page displays? _____
2. Click the Back button on the Standard Buttons toolbar twice. What Web page displays? _____
3. Click the Forward button on the Standard Buttons toolbar bar. What Web page displays? _____

Part 5: *Entering a URL in the Address Bar*

1. Click the URL in the Address bar to highlight the URL.
2. Type www.scsite.com/win2000/ in the Address bar and then press the ENTER key.
3. Click the Steve's Cool Sites hyperlink on the Web page.
4. Click any hyperlinks that are of interest to you. Which hyperlink did you like the best? _____
5. Use the Back button or Forward button to display the Web site you like the best.
6. Click the Print button on the Standard Buttons toolbar to print the Web page.
7. Click the Close button on the Microsoft Internet Explorer title bar.

4 Launching an Application

Instructions: Perform the following steps to launch the Notepad application using the Start menu and create the homework list shown in Figure 1-50. **Notepad** is a popular application program available with Windows 2000 that allows you to create, save, and print simple text documents.

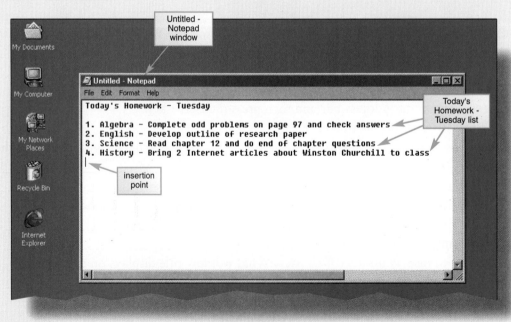

FIGURE 1-50

In the Lab

Part 1: *Launching the Notepad Application*

1. If necessary, start Microsoft Windows 2000.
2. Click the Start button.
3. Point to Programs on the Start menu, point to Accessories on the Programs submenu, and click Notepad on the Accessories submenu. The Untitled - Notepad window displays and an insertion point (flashing vertical line) displays in the blank area below the menu bar.

Part 2: *Creating a Document Using Notepad*

1. Type Today's Homework - Tuesday and then press the ENTER key twice.
2. Type 1. Algebra - Complete odd problems on page 97 and check answers and then press the ENTER key.
3. Type 2. English - Develop outline of research paper and then press the ENTER key.
4. Type 3. Science - Read chapter 12 and do end of chapter questions and then press the ENTER key.
5. Type 4. History - Bring 2 Internet articles about Winston Churchill to class and then press the ENTER key.

Part 3: *Printing the Today's Homework Document*

1. Click File on the menu bar and then click Print. Click the Print button in the Print dialog box to print the document.
2. Retrieve the printed Today's Homework list from the printer.

Part 4: *Closing the Notepad Window*

1. Click the Close button on the Notepad title bar.
2. Click the No button in the Notepad dialog box to not save the Today's Homework document.

Cases and Places

The difficulty of these case studies varies:
◗ are the least difficult; ◗◗ are more difficult; and ◗◗◗ are the most difficult.

1 ◗ Using Windows Help, locate the *Getting Started* online book. Using the online book, read about the following ten topics: Connecting to a Local Area Network, Customizing Your Desktop, Emergency Repair Disk, NTFS File System, Hardware Compatibility List, Microsoft NetMeeting, Active Desktop, Search Tips, Universal Serial Bus (USB), and Watching TV. Select five of the ten topics. In a brief report, summarize the five topics you have selected.

2 ◗ Technical support is an important consideration when installing and using an operating system or an application software program. The ability to obtain a valid answer to a question at the moment you have the question can be the difference between a frustrating experience and a positive experience. Using Windows 2000 Help, the Internet, or another research facility, write a brief report on the options that are available for obtaining help and technical support while using Windows 2000.

3 ◗◗ Microsoft's decision to make the Internet Explorer 5 Web browser part of the Windows 2000 operating system caused many legal problems for Microsoft. Using the Internet, computer magazines and newspapers, or other resources, prepare a brief report on these legal problems. Explain the arguments for and against combining the browser and operating system. Identify the key players on both sides of the legal battle and summarize the final decision. Did the legal process or final decision affect the release date and contents of Windows 2000? Do you think computer users benefited from this decision? Explain your answers.

4 ◗◗◗ In addition to Windows 2000, Microsoft also sells the Windows 98 operating system. Some say Windows 2000 will replace Windows 98 in the future. Using the Internet, computer magazines, or other resources, prepare a brief report comparing and contrasting the operating systems. How do their graphical user interfaces compare? What features and commands are shared by both operating systems? Does either operating system have features or commands that the other operating system does not have? Explain whether you think Windows 2000 could replace Windows 98.

5 ◗◗◗ Because of the many important tasks an operating system performs, most businesses put a great deal of thought into choosing an operating system. Interview a person at a local business about the operating system it uses with its computers. Based on the interview, write a brief report on why the business chose that operating system, how satisfied it is with it, and under what circumstances it may consider switching to a different operating system.

Microsoft Windows 2000

Using Windows Explorer

PROJECT

2

OBJECTIVES

You will have mastered the material in this project when you can:

- Launch Windows Explorer
- Identify the elements of the Exploring window
- Display the contents of a folder
- Expand and collapse a folder
- Select and copy one file or a group of files
- Create, rename, and delete a folder
- Rename and delete a file
- Quit Windows Explorer and shut down Windows 2000

Desktop Explorer

Navigating Resources and Networks

The great explorers from Portugal, Spain, Italy, France, and England ventured farther with each voyage, spanning the globe in the face of great peril. It is only through the expanse of time that the great undertakings of the seafarers and their everyday woes can be understood completely. In the fifteenth and sixteenth centuries, northern voyagers such as Jacques Cartier and John Davis endured great hardship in contrast to the mild winds Columbus experienced in the southerly passages. From the navigators' perspective, an Atlantic crossing was simple.

In rough seas, anything might happen to mariners in the North Atlantic. Gales from the west hurled giant waves against vessels; easterly gusts soaked the sailors with freezing rain; brutal northerly winds cracked masts and split sails. Many died on these northern journeys.

After Christopher Columbus's return to Spain from the famous 1492 voyage across the Atlantic, other European explorers began navigating to North America. In 1497, John Cabot explored the coasts of Labrador, Newfoundland, and New England. Juan Ponce de León discovered Florida and part of the Yucatán Peninsula in the early 1500s. Hernán Cortés invaded Mexico in 1519 and then conquered the Aztecs.

Every age has produced those who have an insatiable thirst for knowing what lies over the next hill: Sir Edmund Hillary, Junípero Serra, Louis Joliet, Amelia Earhart, Vasco Nuñez de Balboa, Sir Walter Raleigh, and Leif Ericsson. The list of familiar names seems endless. In the latter half of the twentieth century, Neil Armstrong and Buzz Aldrin led the way to the Moon, Jacques Cousteau explored the wonders beneath the sea, and Robert Ballard discovered the resting place of the *Titanic*.

The names of the crafts in the trek toward the stars are legendary in themselves: *Apollo, Sputnik, Explorer, Voyager, Mir,* the *Mars Pathfinder*. These and many others have spun the first fibers of a golden rope that may lift humankind to Mars and beyond in the twenty-first century.

The increasing power and versatility of modern personal computers have given people the means to embark on these and other grand individual adventures.

Yet, the progressive complexity of these systems can dissuade many from achieving the necessary skills to manage their work effectively. Windows Explorer, an application program included with Windows 2000, allows you to manage files on a network, as well as your own computer. In this project you will use Windows Explorer and the My Computer window to select and copy a group of files between drives; copy and move files and folders; and create, rename, and delete files on a floppy disk. Knowledge of these common operations offers efficiency in organizing your work.

As a desktop explorer of the twenty-first century, you have the tools to navigate computer and network resources at the click of a mouse button using the best of the Windows operating systems developed to date.

Microsoft Windows 2000

Using Windows Explorer

P R O J E C T
2

CASE PERSPECTIVE

Your organization has installed a Microsoft Windows 2000 network. In the process, the organization will upgrade the operating system on each computer to Microsoft Windows 2000 Professional. Your supervisor has read in computer magazines that to use Windows 2000 effectively, people must learn Windows 2000 Explorer. Although almost everyone is excited about the change, those who have little experience using Windows 2000 are apprehensive about having to learn to manage files. Your supervisor asks you to teach a class with an emphasis on file management to all employees who are not experienced using Windows. Your goal is to become competent using Windows 2000 Explorer so you can teach the class.

Introduction

Windows Explorer is an application program included with Windows 2000 that allows you to view the contents of the computer, the hierarchy of folders on the computer, and the files and folders in each folder.

Windows Explorer also allows you to organize the files and folders on the computer by copying and moving the files and folders. In this project, you will use Windows Explorer to work with the files and folders on the computer; select and copy a group of files between the hard drive and a floppy disk; create, rename, and delete a folder on a floppy disk; and rename and delete a file on a floppy disk. These are common operations that you should understand how to perform.

Launching Microsoft Windows 2000

As explained in Project 1, when you turn on the computer, an introductory screen containing the words, Microsoft Windows 2000 Professional, and the Please Wait... screen display momentarily followed by the Welcome to Windows dialog box containing the instructions to begin the log on process (Press CTRL+ALT+ DELETE to begin.). Holding down the CTRL key and pressing the ALT and DELETE keys simultaneously closes the Welcome to Windows dialog box and displays the Log On to Windows dialog box. Entering a user name and password and then clicking the OK button logs you on to the computer, closes the Log On to Windows dialog box, clears the screen, and displays several items on the desktop.

If the Getting Started with Windows 2000 window displays on the desktop, click the Close button on the title bar to close the window. Five icons (My Documents, My Computer, My Network Places, Recycle Bin, and Internet Explorer) display along the left edge of the desktop and the taskbar displays along the bottom (Figure 2-1). The icons may be different on your computer.

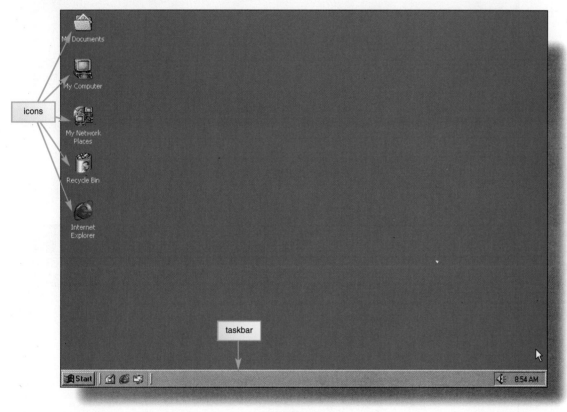

FIGURE 2-1

Launching Windows Explorer and Maximizing Its Window

As with many operations, Windows 2000 offers a variety of ways to launch Windows Explorer. To launch Windows Explorer using the My Computer icon, complete the steps on the next page.

To Launch Windows Explorer and Maximize Its Window

1 **Right-click the My Computer icon on the desktop and then point to Explore on the shortcut menu.**

Windows highlights the My Computer icon and displays a shortcut menu (Figure 2-2). Clicking the highlighted Explore command will launch Windows 2000 Explorer.

FIGURE 2-2

2 **Click Explore and then click the Maximize button on the My Computer title bar.**

The maximized My Computer window displays and the taskbar button area contains the recessed My Computer button (Figure 2-3).

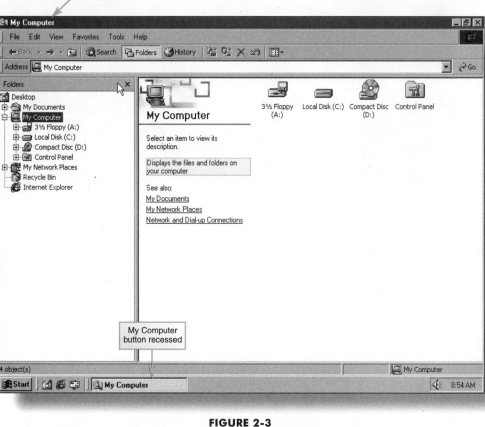

FIGURE 2-3

Other **Ways**

1. Right-click Start button or any icon on desktop (except Internet Explorer), click Explore on shortcut menu
2. Click Start button, point to Programs, point to Accessories, click Windows Explorer
3. Double-click My Computer icon, click Folders button on Standard Buttons toolbar

Windows Explorer

When you launch Windows Explorer by right-clicking the My Computer icon, the
My Computer window displays (Figure 2-4). The menu bar contains the File, Edit,
View, Favorites, Tools, and Help menu names. These menus contain commands to
organize and work with the drives on the computer and the files and folders on those
drives. Below the menu bar is the Standard Buttons toolbar and Address bar. The
recessed Folders button displays on the Standard Buttons toolbar and the My
Computer icon and folder name display on the Address bar.

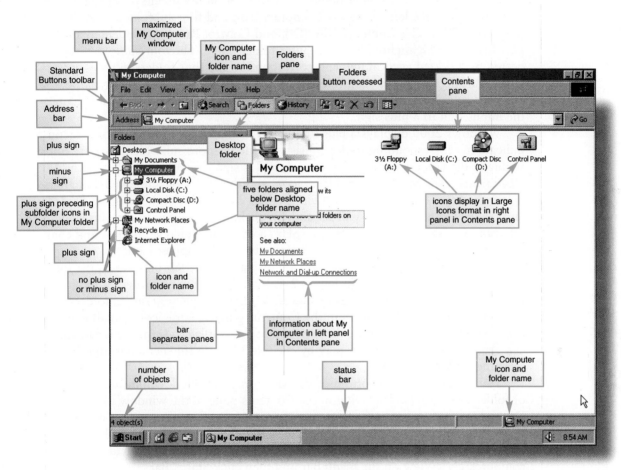

FIGURE 2-4

The main window consists of two panes separated by a bar. The left pane of
the window, called the **Folders pane**, is identified by the Folders title and contains a
hierarchy of folders on the computer. The recessed Folders button on the Standard
Buttons toolbar indicates the Folder pane displays in the My Computer window. The
right pane of the window, called the **Contents pane,** contains two panels. The left
panel contains information about My Computer and the right panel contains the
contents of the My Computer folder (3½ Floppy (A:), Local Disk (C:), Compact
Disc (D:), and Control Panel icons). The icons in the right panel may be different on
your computer.

A message on the left of the status bar located at the bottom of the window indicates the right panel in the Contents pane contains four objects. A message on the
right of the status bar contains the My Computer icon and folder name. You can
change the size of the Folders pane and Contents pane by dragging the bar that
separates the two panes.

An icon and folder name represent each folder in the Folders pane. The first folder, consisting of an icon and the Desktop folder name, represents the desktop of the computer. The five folders indented and aligned below the Desktop folder name (My Documents, My Computer, My Network Places, Recycle Bin, and Internet Explorer) connect to the vertical line below the Desktop icon. These folders correspond to the five icons displayed on the left edge of the desktop (see Figure 2-1 on page WIN 2.5). The folders shown on your computer may be different.

Windows 2000 displays a **minus sign** (–) in a small box to the left of an icon in the Folders pane to indicate the corresponding folder contains one or more folders that are visible in the Folders pane. These folders, called **subfolders**, are indented and aligned below each folder name. In Figure 2-4 on the previous page, a minus sign displays to the left of the My Computer icon and four subfolders (3½ Floppy (A:), Local Disk (C:), Compact Disc (D:), and Control Panel) are indented and display below the highlighted My Computer folder name. The four subfolders are connected by a dotted vertical line and correspond to the four folders in the Contents pane. Clicking the minus sign, referred to as **collapsing the folder**, removes the indented subfolders from the hierarchy of folders in the Folders pane and changes the minus sign to a plus sign.

Windows 2000 displays a **plus sign** (+) in a small box to the left of an icon to indicate the corresponding folder consists of one or more subfolders that are not visible in the Folders pane. In Figure 2-4, a plus sign displays to the left of the My Documents icon, My Network Places icon, and the four icons indented and aligned below the My Computer icon (3½ Floppy (A:), Local Disk (C:), Compact Disc (D:), and Control Panel). As you will see shortly, clicking the box with the plus sign, referred to as **expanding the folder**, displays a list of indented subfolders and changes the plus sign to a minus sign as shown with the My Computer icon.

If neither a plus sign nor a minus sign displays to the left of an icon, the folder does not contain subfolders. In Figure 2-4, the Recycle Bin and Internet Explorer icons are not preceded by a plus or minus sign and do not contain subfolders.

You can display the folders in the Contents pane as large icons, small icons, a list, or with details. Currently, the files and folder display in **Large Icons format**. You can change how the folders display by clicking View on the menu bar and then selecting the icon format.

The status bar at the bottom of the My Computer window indicates the number of folders, or objects, displaying in the Contents pane of the window (4 object(s)). Depending on the objects displaying in the Contents pane, the amount of disk space the objects occupy and the amount of unused disk space also may display on the status bar. If the status bar does not display in the My Computer window on your computer, click View on the menu bar and then click Status Bar.

In addition to using Windows Explorer to explore My Computer by right-clicking the My Computer icon, you also can use Windows Explorer to explore different aspects of the computer by right-clicking the Start button on the taskbar and the My Documents, My Network Places, and Recycle Bin icons on the desktop.

Displaying the Contents of a Folder

In Figure 2-4, Explorer displays the hierarchy of items in the Folders pane and then displays information about and the contents of the My Computer folder in the Contents pane. To display the contents of another folder, click the folder name in the Folders pane in the window. Perform the following steps to display the contents of the Local Disk (C:) folder.

Steps To Display the Contents of a Folder

1 Point to the Local Disk (C:) icon in the Folders pane (Figure 2-5).

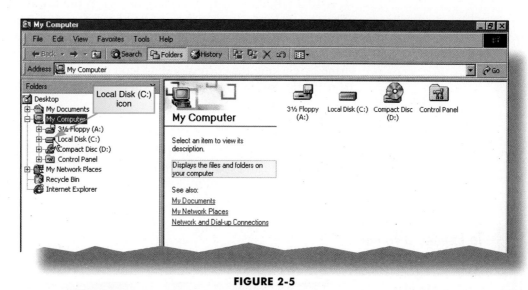

FIGURE 2-5

2 Click the Local Disk (C:) icon.

The window title, Address bar, and taskbar button contain the new Local Disk (C:) folder name and the highlighted Local Disk (C:) folder name displays in the Folders pane (Figure 2-6). The Contents pane contains information about the Local Disk (C:) folder and the contents of the Local Disk (C:) folder. Folder icons display first in the Contents pane and then the file icons. The contents of your Local Disk (C:) folder may be different.

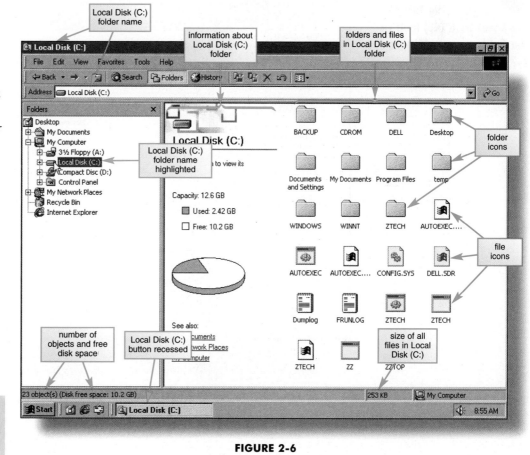

FIGURE 2-6

Other Ways

1. Press DOWN ARROW to select Local Disk (C:) folder name in Folders pane
2. Press TAB to select any folder name in Contents pane, use ARROW keys to select Local Disk (C:) folder name
3. Double-click Local Disk (C:) icon in Contents pane

The status bar messages shown in Figure 2-6 on the previous page indicate 23 objects display in the Contents pane, the amount of unused (free) disk space on drive C is 10.2 GB, and the total size of all files in the Local Disk (C:) folder is 253 KB. The objects in the Contents pane may be different on your computer.

In addition to displaying information about the Local Disk (C:) folder and its contents, you can display similar information about the other folders in the Folders pane by clicking the corresponding icon or folder name. The information and contents of the folder you click then will display in the Contents pane.

Expanding a Folder

When a plus sign in a small box displays to the left of a folder icon in the Folders pane, you can expand the folder to show all the subfolders it contains. To expand drive C and view the subfolders, complete the following steps.

Steps To Expand a Folder

① Point to the plus sign to the left of the Local Disk (C:) icon in the Folders pane (Figure 2-7).

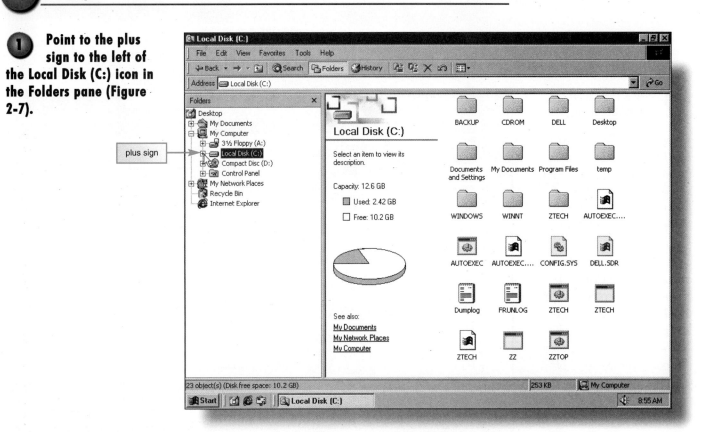

FIGURE 2-7

2 Click the plus sign.

A minus sign replaces the plus sign to the left of the Local Disk (C:) icon and the hierarchy below the Local Disk (C:) icon expands to display the subfolders in the Local Disk (C:) folder (Figure 2-8). Your subfolders may be different.

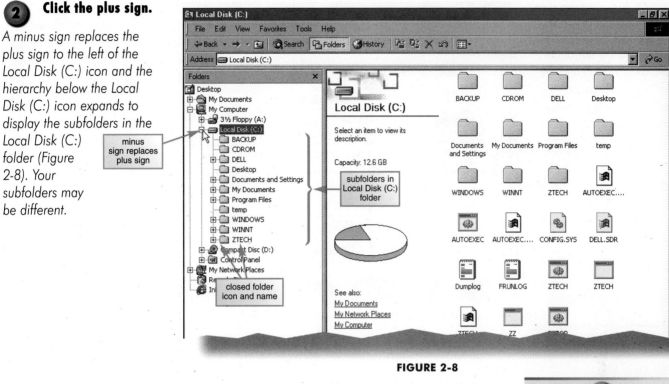

FIGURE 2-8

The subfolders in the expanded Local Disk (C:) folder shown in Figure 2-8 are indented and aligned below the highlighted Local Disk (C:) folder name. A closed folder icon and folder name identify each subfolder in the Local Disk (C:) folder.

Collapsing a Folder

Currently, the subfolders in the Local Disk (C:) folder display indented and aligned below the Local Disk (C:) folder name (see Figure 2-8). Windows 2000 displays a minus sign to the left of the Local Disk (C:) icon to indicate the folder is expanded. To collapse the Local Disk (C:) folder and remove its subfolders from view in the hierarchy of folders in the Folders pane, perform the following steps.

Other Ways

1. Double-click folder icon in Folders pane
2. Select folder, press PLUS SIGN on numeric keypad
3. Select folder, press RIGHT ARROW

Steps To Collapse a Folder

1 Point to the minus sign to the left of the Local Disk (C:) icon in the Folders pane (Figure 2-9).

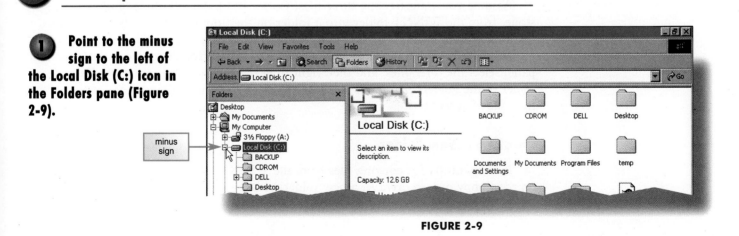

FIGURE 2-9

Click the minus sign.

A plus sign replaces the minus sign to the left of the Local Disk (C:) icon and the subfolders in the Local Disk (C:) folder are removed from the hierarchy of folders (Figure 2-10).

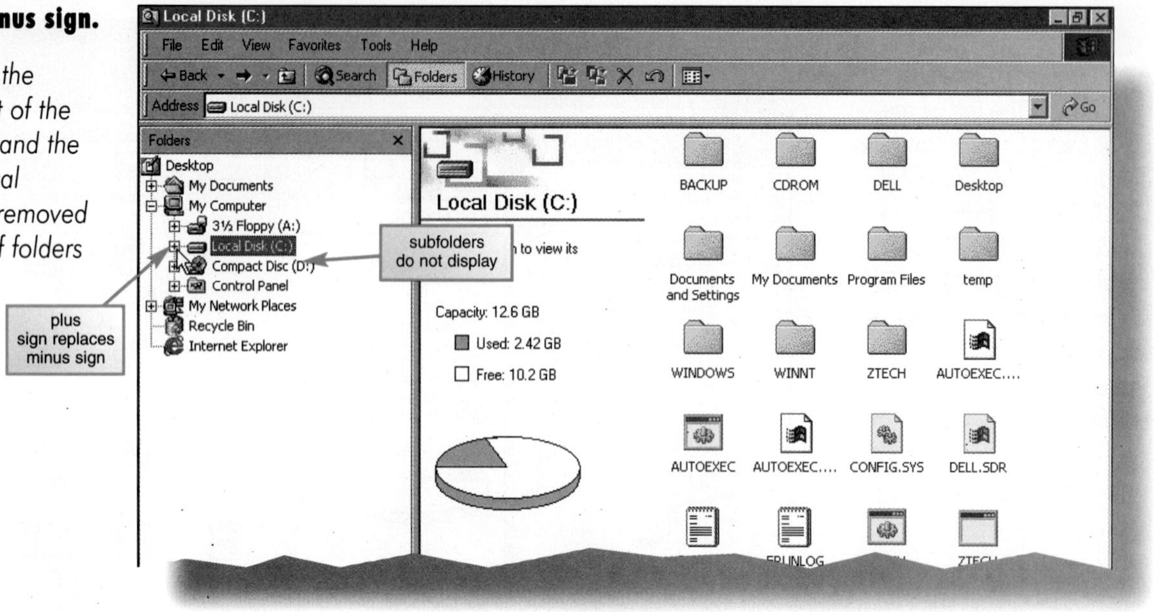

plus sign replaces minus sign

FIGURE 2-10

Knowing how to display the contents of a folder, expand a folder, and collapse a folder are important skills. You will find that you use Explorer to perform a significant amount of file maintenance on the computer.

Copying Files to a Folder on a Floppy Disk

One common operation that every student should understand is copying a file or group of files from one disk to another disk or from one folder to another folder. In the following sections, you will create a new folder named My Files on the floppy disk in drive A, select a group of files in the WINNT folder on drive C, and then copy the files from the WINNT folder on drive C to the My Files folder on drive A.

When copying files, the drive and folder containing the files to be copied are called the **source drive** and **source folder**, respectively. The drive and folder to which the files are copied are called the **destination drive** and **destination folder,** respectively. The WINNT folder is the source folder, drive C is the source drive, the My Files folder is the destination folder, and drive A is the destination drive.

Assume you want to copy three files, Coffee Bean, Gone Fishing, and Greenstone, from the WINNT folder into a folder on the floppy disk in drive A. To copy the files, you must create the My Files folder on drive A, display the 3½ Floppy (A:) folder in the Folders pane, display the contents of the WINNT folder in the Contents pane, select the three files, and then right-drag the selected files to the My Files folder in the Folders pane. The steps to follow to copy the three files are contained in the following sections.

Creating a New Folder

In preparation for copying files from the WINNT folder on drive C to a folder on the floppy disk in drive A, a new folder with the name of My Files will be created on the floppy disk. Perform the following steps to create the new folder.

To Create a New Folder

1 Insert a formatted floppy disk into drive A on the computer.

2 Click the 3½ Floppy (A:) icon in the Folders pane and then point to an open area of the Contents pane.

The highlighted 3½ Floppy (A:) folder name displays in the Folders pane, information about and the contents of the empty 3½ Floppy (A:) folder display in the Contents pane, and the status bar messages change (Figure 2-11). The 3½ Floppy (A:) folder name displays on the title bar, Address bar, and taskbar button. The files and folders may be different on your computer.

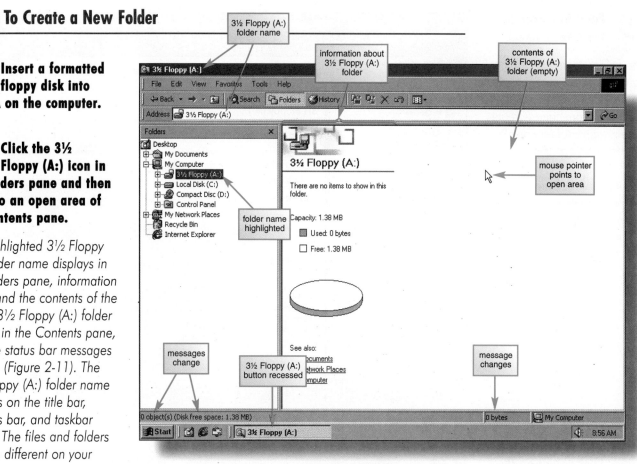

FIGURE 2-11

3 Right-click the open area and then point to New on the shortcut menu.

A shortcut menu, containing the highlighted New command, and the New submenu display in the Contents pane (Figure 2-12). Although no subfolders display in the Contents pane and a plus sign displays to the left of the 3½ Floppy (A:) icon in the Folders pane, a plus sign displays to the left of the icon.

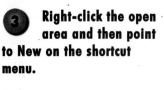

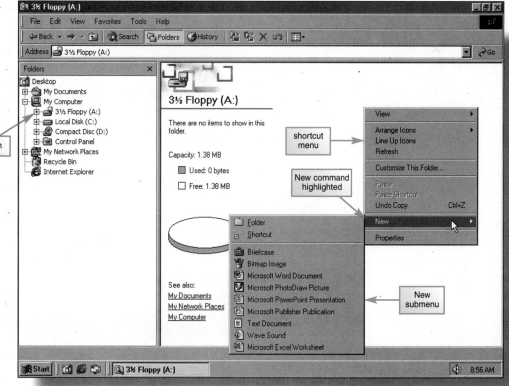

FIGURE 2-12

4 **Point to Folder on the New submenu.**

The Folder command is highlighted on the New submenu and a message describing the Folder command (Creates a new, empty folder.) displays on the status bar (Figure 2-13). Clicking the Folder command will create a folder on the floppy disk in drive A using the default folder name, New Folder, and display the New Folder icon in the Contents pane.

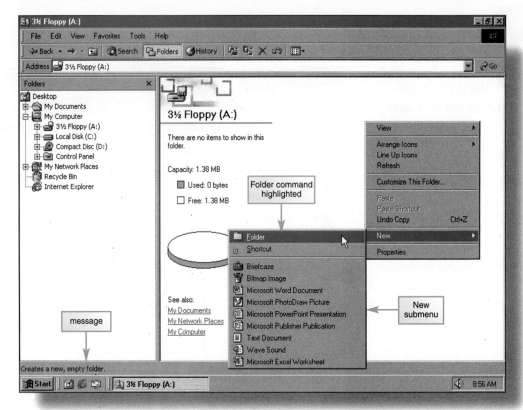

FIGURE 2-13

5 **Click Folder on the New submenu.**

The shortcut menu and New submenu close (Figure 2-14). Information about the new folder and the New Folder icon display in the Contents pane. The text box below the icon contains the highlighted default folder name, New Folder, and an insertion point. The plus sign to the left of the 3½ Floppy (A:) icon in the Folders pane indicates the 3½ Floppy (A:) folder contains a subfolder. A status bar message indicates one object is selected.

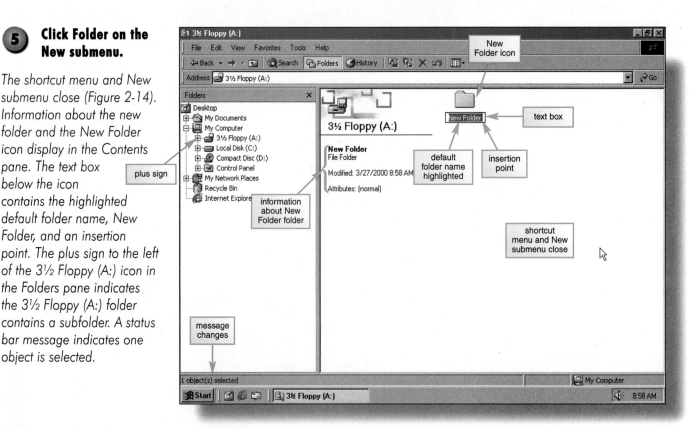

FIGURE 2-14

6 **Type** My Files **in the text box and then press the ENTER key.**

The new folder name, My Files, is entered in the text box and the text box is removed (Figure 2-15). The My Files folder name displays in the left panel in the Contents pane.

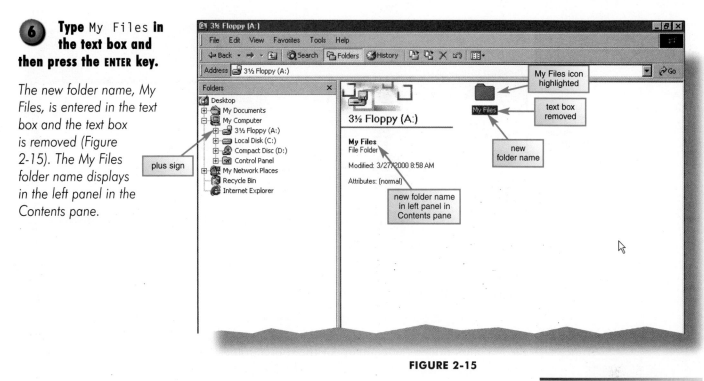

FIGURE 2-15

After creating the My Files folder on the floppy disk in drive A, you can save files in the folder or copy files from other folders to that folder. In the following section, you will copy the group of files consisting of the Coffee Bean, Gone Fishing, and Greenstone files from the WINNT folder on drive C to the My Files folder on drive A.

Displaying the Destination Folder

To copy the Coffee Bean, Gone Fishing, and Greenstone files from the WINNT folder on drive C to the My Files folder on drive A, the three files will be selected in the Contents pane and right-dragged to the My Files folder in the Folders pane. Prior to selecting or right-dragging the files, the My Files folder (destination folder) on drive A must be visible in the Folders pane and the three files to be copied must be visible in the Contents pane.

Currently, the plus sign to the left of the 3½ Floppy (A:) icon indicates the folder contains one or more subfolders that are not visible in the Folders pane (see Figure 2-15). Perform the following steps to expand the 3½ Floppy (A:) folder in the Folders pane to display the My Files subfolder.

TO EXPAND A FOLDER

1 Point to the plus sign to the left of the 3½ Floppy (A:) icon in the Folders pane.

2 Click the plus sign to display the subfolders in the 3½ Floppy (A:) folder.

In the Folders pane, a minus sign replaces the plus sign to the left of the 3½ Floppy (A:) folder icon, the 3½ Floppy (A:) folder name is highlighted, and the My Files subfolder displays in the 3½ Floppy (A:) folder, indented and aligned below the highlighted 3½ Floppy (A:) folder name (Figure 2-16 on the next page).

Other Ways

1. Select folder icon in Folders pane, on File menu point to New, click Folder, type folder name, press ENTER key

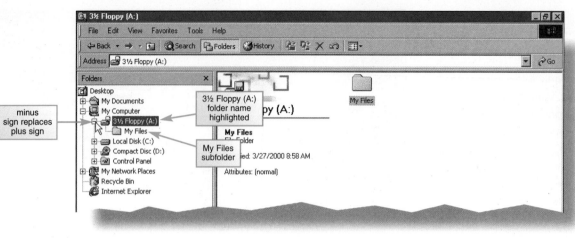

FIGURE 2-16

Displaying the Contents of a Subfolder

Currently, the My Files folder displays in the Contents pane in the 3½ Floppy (A:) window. To copy the files from the source folder (WINNT folder on drive C) to the My Files folder, the contents of the source folder must be visible in the Contents pane. To make the contents of the WINNT folder visible, you must expand the Local Disk (C:) folder in the Folders pane and then click the WINNT folder name to display the contents in the Contents pane. Perform the following steps to display the contents of the WINNT subfolder in the Contents pane.

Steps To Display the Contents of a Subfolder

1 **Click the plus sign to the left of the Local Disk (C:) icon in the Folders pane and then point to the WINNT icon.**

A minus sign replaces the plus sign to the left of the Local Disk (C:) icon, the Local Disk (C:) folder expands, and its subfolders display (Figure 2-17). The WINNT folder contains a collection of files, called **clip art files***, each of which contains a graphic image.*

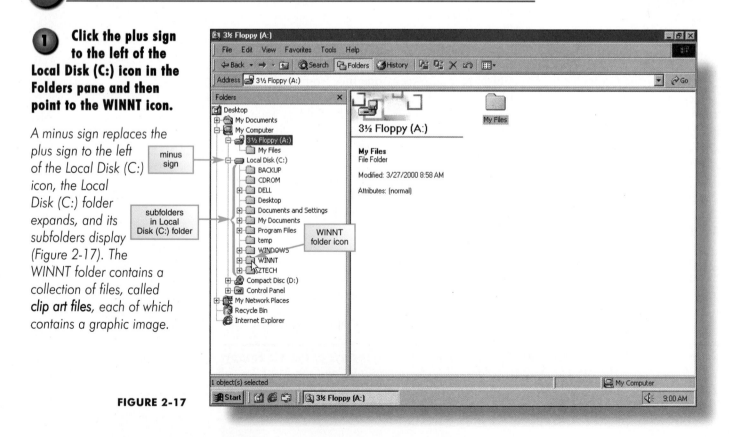

FIGURE 2-17

2 **Click the WINNT icon and then point to the Show Files link in the Contents pane.**

The WINNT folder name is highlighted in the Folders pane, the closed folder icon to the left of the WINNT folder name changes to an open folder icon, and the Contents pane contains information about the WINNT folder, including a warning message, the Show Files link, and a graphic image (Figure 2-18). Pointing to the Show Files link causes the mouse pointer to change to a hand icon.

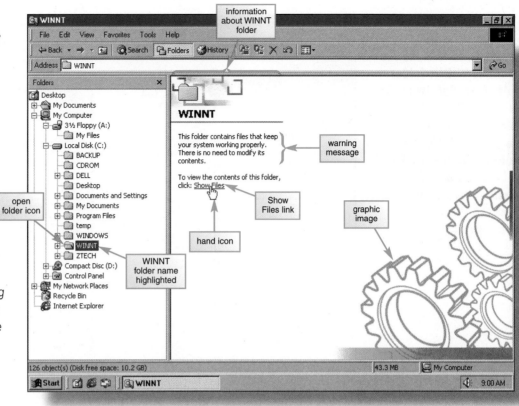

FIGURE 2-18

3 **Click Show Files.**

The WINNT folder name is no longer highlighted in the Folders pane and a partial list of the folders in the WINNT folder replaces the graphic image in the Contents pane (Figure 2-19). Additional folders and files display when you scroll the right panel in the Contents pane.

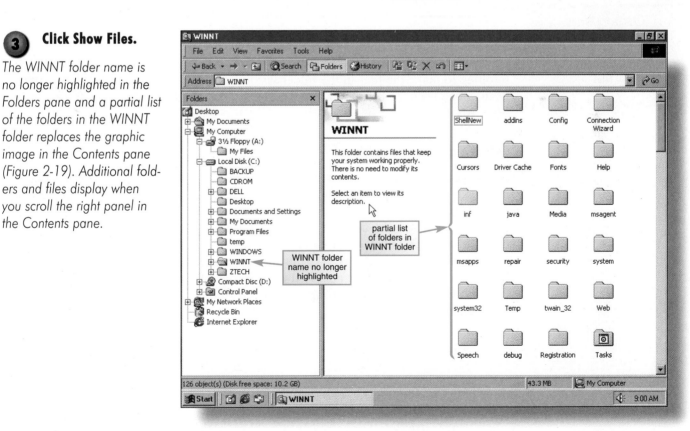

FIGURE 2-19

Scroll the right panel in the Contents pane to make the files in the WINNT folder visible. A partial list of the files in the WINNT folder display in the Contents pane (Figure 2-20). The files in the WINNT folder may be different and file extensions may display as part of the file names on your computer.

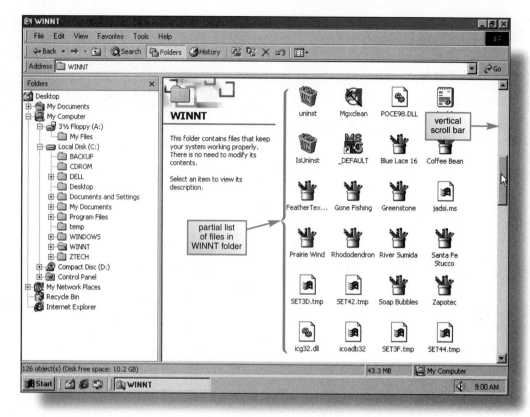

FIGURE 2-20

Other Ways

1. Double-click Local Disk (C:) icon, click WINNT icon, click Show Files

After displaying the contents of the WINNT folder in the Contents pane and scrolling to make the files in the folder visible, you will select the three files (Coffee Bean, Gone Fishing, and Greenstone) and copy the files to the My Files folder on drive A.

Selecting a Group of Files

It is easy to copy a single file or group of files from one folder to another folder using Windows Explorer. To copy a single file, click the file icon or name in the Contents pane to select it and then right-drag the highlighted file to the folder icon in the Folders pane where the file is to be copied. Grouped files are copied in a similar fashion by clicking the icon or name of the first file in a group of files to select it. You select the remaining files in the group by pointing to each file icon or name, holding down the CTRL key, and then clicking the file icon or file name. Perform the following steps to select the group of files consisting of the Coffee Bean, Gone Fishing, and Greenstone files.

To Select a Group of Files

1 **Select the Coffee Bean file by clicking the Coffee Bean icon and then point to the Gone Fishing icon.**

Information about the Coffee Bean file, an image of the Coffee Bean file, and the highlighted Coffee Bean file display in the Contents pane (Figure 2-21). Messages on the status bar indicate the file type (Bitmap Image) and file size (16.6 KB) of the Coffee Bean file.

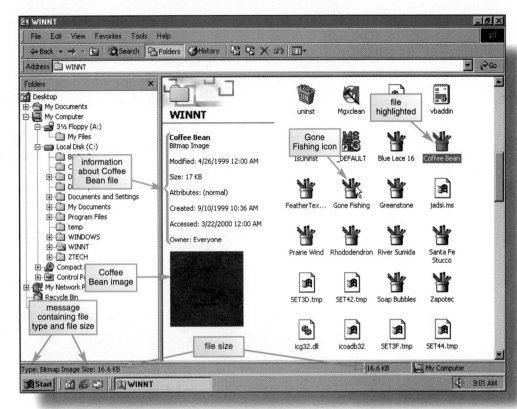

FIGURE 2-21

2 **Hold down the CTRL key, click the Gone Fishing icon, release the CTRL key, and then point to the Greenstone icon.**

The number of files selected, total size of both files, file names, and the highlighted Coffee Bean and Gone Fishing files display in the Contents pane (Figure 2-22). Status bar messages indicate two objects are selected in the Contents pane and the file size (in kilobytes) of the two objects.

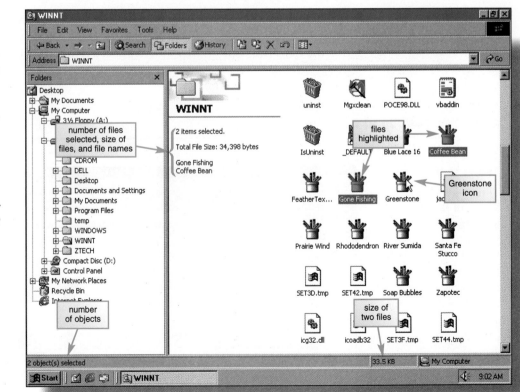

FIGURE 2-22

3 Hold down the CTRL key, click the Greenstone icon, and then release the CTRL key.

The number of files selected, total size of the three files, file names, and the highlighted group of files consisting of the Coffee Bean, Gone Fishing, and Greenstone files display in the Contents pane (Figure 2-23). Status bar messages indicate three objects are selected in the Contents pane and the size (in kilobytes) of the three objects.

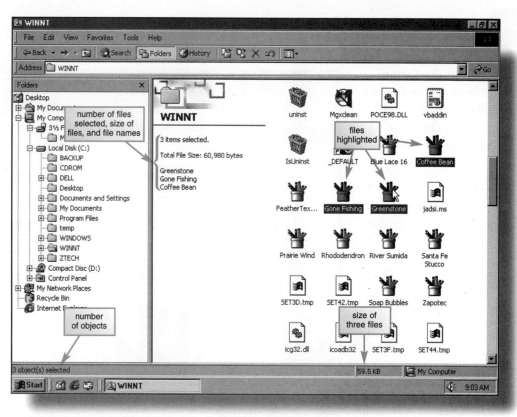

FIGURE 2-23

Other Ways

1. To select contiguous files, select first file icon, hold down SHIFT key, click last file icon
2. To select all files, on Edit menu click Select All
3. Press CTRL+A

Copying a Group of Files

After selecting a group of files, copy the files to the My Files folder on drive A by pointing to any highlighted icon in the Contents pane and right-dragging the icon over the My Files icon in the Folders pane. Perform the following steps to copy a group of files.

Steps **To Copy a Group of Files**

1 Point to the highlighted Coffee Bean file icon in the Contents pane.

The mouse pointer points to the highlighted Coffee Bean icon in the Contents pane and the My Files folder icon is visible in the Folders pane (Figure 2-24).

FIGURE 2-24

Right-drag the Coffee Bean icon on top of the My Files icon, release the right mouse button, and then point to Copy Here on the shortcut menu.

As you right-drag the icon, a dimmed image of the three icons displays and the My Files folder name is highlighted. When you release the right mouse, a shortcut menu displays and the Copy Here command on the shortcut menu is highlighted (Figure 2-25).

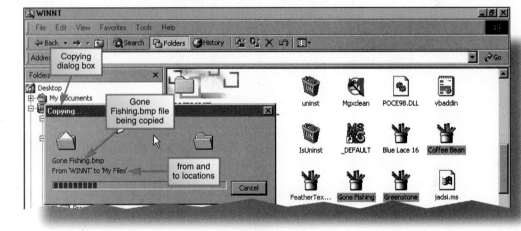

FIGURE 2-25

Click Copy Here.

The Copying dialog box displays and remains on the screen while each file is copied to the My Files folder (Figure 2-26). The Copying dialog box shown in Figure 2-26 indicates that Windows 2000 is copying the Gone Fishing.bmp file from the WINNT folder to the My Files folder.

FIGURE 2-26

Displaying the Contents of the My Files Folder

After copying a group of files, verify that the files were copied into the correct folder. To view the files that were copied to the My Files folder, perform the steps on the next page.

Other Ways

1. Drag file icon from Contents pane to folder icon in Folders pane
2. Select files to copy in Contents pane, click Copy To button on Standard Buttons toolbar, select folder to receive copy, click OK button
3. Select files to copy in Contents pane, on Edit menu click Copy, select folder icon to receive copy, on Edit menu click Paste
4. Select files to copy, press CTRL+C, select folder icon to receive copy, press CTRL+V

TO DISPLAY THE CONTENTS OF A FOLDER

1 Point to the My Files icon in the Folders pane.

2 Click the My Files icon.

The highlighted My Files folder name displays in the Folders pane, the open folder icon replaces the closed folder icon to the left of the My Files icon, the contents of the My Files folder display in the Contents pane, and the message on the status bar changes (Figure 2-27). The status bar messages indicate three objects display in the Contents pane, 1.33MB of free disk space is available on the disk in drive A, and the size of the three files is 59.5 KB.

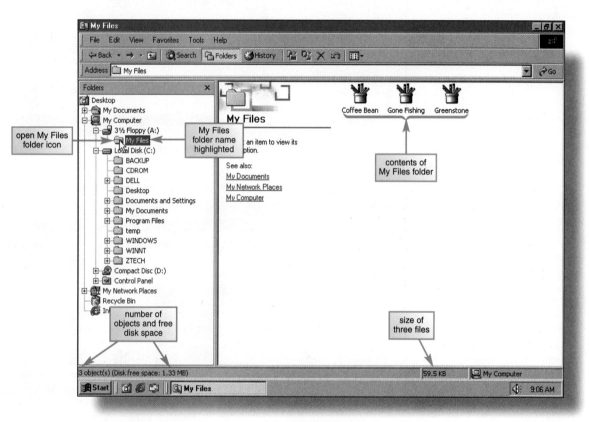

FIGURE 2-27

Renaming a File or Folder

In some circumstances, you may want to rename a file or a folder. You may want to distinguish a file in one folder from a copy, or you may decide you need a better name to identify the file. To change the name of the Gone Fishing file in the My Files folder on drive A to Gone Fly Fishing, complete the following steps.

Steps To Rename a File

1 **Right-click the Gone Fishing icon in the right panel of the Contents pane and then point to Rename on the shortcut menu.**

Information about the Gone Fishing file, an image of the file, the highlighted Gone Fishing icon, and a shortcut menu display in the Contents pane (Figure 2-28). A message describing the Rename command (Renames the selected item.) displays on the status bar.

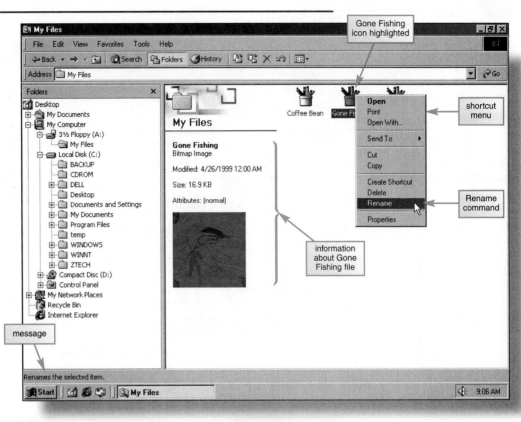

FIGURE 2-28

2 **Click Rename. Type** Gone Fly Fishing **and then press the ENTER key.**

The file is renamed Gone Fly Fishing (Figure 2-29). Note that the file in the 3½ Floppy (A:) folder on drive A is renamed, but the original file in the WINNT folder on drive C is not renamed.

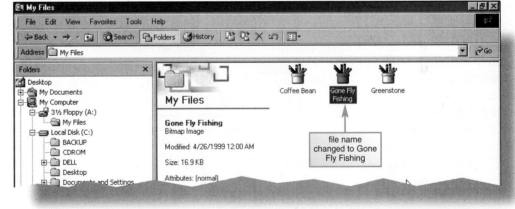

FIGURE 2-29

You can rename files on a hard disk using the same technique, but use caution when doing so. If you inadvertently rename a file that is associated with certain programs, the programs may not be able to find the file and, therefore, may not work properly.

You also may want to rename a folder. For example, you may want to change the name of the My Files folder on drive A to Clip Art Files because the folder contains clip art files. To accomplish this, complete the steps on the next page.

Other Ways

1. Click file name twice (do not double-click file name), type file name, press ENTER
2. Click icon, press F2, type file name, press ENTER
3. Click icon, on File menu click Rename, type file name, press ENTER
4. Select icon, press ALT+F, press M, type file name, press ENTER

Steps **To Rename a Folder**

1 Right-click the My Files folder icon in the Folders pane and then point to Rename on the shortcut menu.

The highlighted My Files folder name and a shortcut menu display in the Folders pane (Figure 2-30).

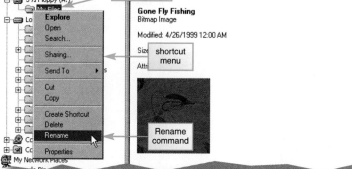

FIGURE 2-30

2 Click Rename. Type Clip Art Files and then press the ENTER key.

The name of the My Files folder in the Folders pane changes to Clip Art Files (Figure 2-31). The new folder name replaces the old folder name in the window title, Address bar, Contents pane, and on the button in the taskbar button area. A message (Done) on the status bar indicates the renaming task is complete.

Other **Ways**

1. Click folder name twice (do not double-click folder name), type folder name, press ENTER

2. Click icon, press F2, type folder name, press ENTER

3. Click icon, on File menu click Rename, type folder name, press ENTER

4. Select icon, press ALT+F, press M, type folder name, press ENTER

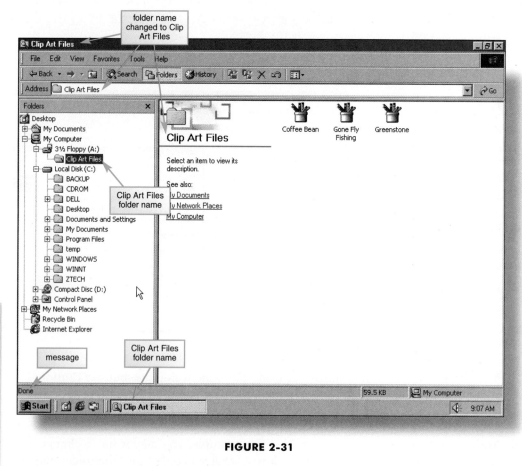

FIGURE 2-31

Deleting a File or Folder

When you no longer need a file or folder, you can delete it. Two methods commonly are used to delete a file or folder. One method uses the Delete command on the shortcut menu that displays when you right-click the file or folder icon. Another method involves right-dragging the unneeded file or folder to the Recycle Bin. The Recycle Bin icon is located at the left edge of the desktop (see Figure 2-1 on page WIN 2.5).

When you delete a file or folder on the hard drive using the Recycle Bin, Windows 2000 temporarily stores the deleted file or folder in the Recycle Bin until you permanently discard the contents by emptying the Recycle Bin. Until the Recycle Bin is emptied, you can retrieve the files and folders you have deleted previously by mistake or other reasons. Keep in mind that unlike deleting files or folders on the hard drive, when you delete a file or folder located on a floppy disk, Windows 2000 deletes the file or folder immediately and does not store the file or folder in the Recycle Bin.

On the following pages, you will delete the Greenstone and Coffee Bean files. The Greenstone file will be deleted by right-clicking and the Coffee Bean file will be deleted by right-dragging the file to the Recycle Bin.

Deleting a File by Right-Clicking Its Icon

Deleting a file by right-clicking its icon produces a shortcut menu that contains the Delete command. To illustrate how to delete a file by right-clicking, perform the following steps to delete the Greenstone file.

Steps To Delete a File by Right-Clicking

1 Right-click the Greenstone icon in the Contents pane and then point to the Delete command on the shortcut menu.

Information about the Greenstone file, an image of the file, the highlighted Greenstone file, and a shortcut menu display in the Contents pane (Figure 2-32). The Clip Art Files folder name in the Folders pane is no longer highlighted. A message describing the Delete command (Deletes the selected items.) displays on the status bar.

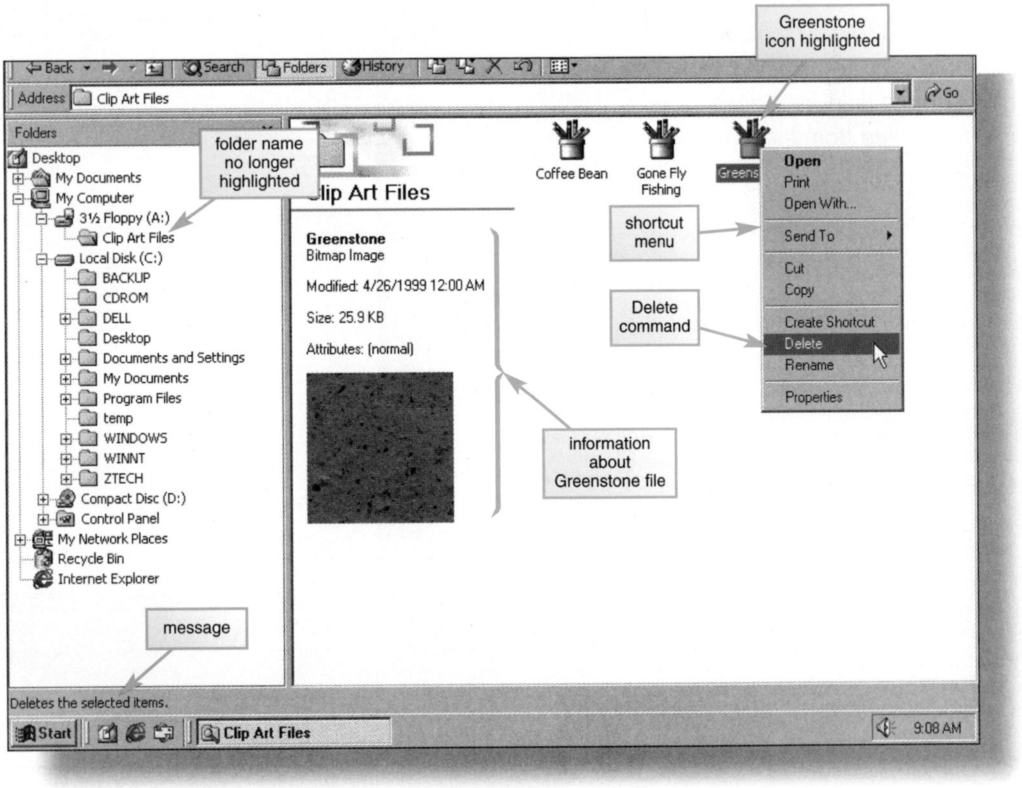

FIGURE 2-32

2 Click Delete. When the Confirm File Delete dialog box displays, point to the Yes button.

The Confirm File Delete dialog box displays (Figure 2-33). The dialog box contains the message, Are you sure you want to delete 'Greenstone'?, and the Yes and No buttons.

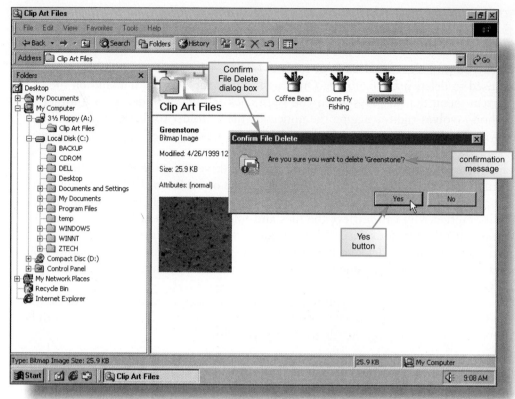

FIGURE 2-33

3 Click the Yes button.

The Confirm File Delete dialog box closes, a Deleting dialog box displays momentarily while the file is being deleted, and the Greenstone file is removed from the Contents pane (Figure 2-34).

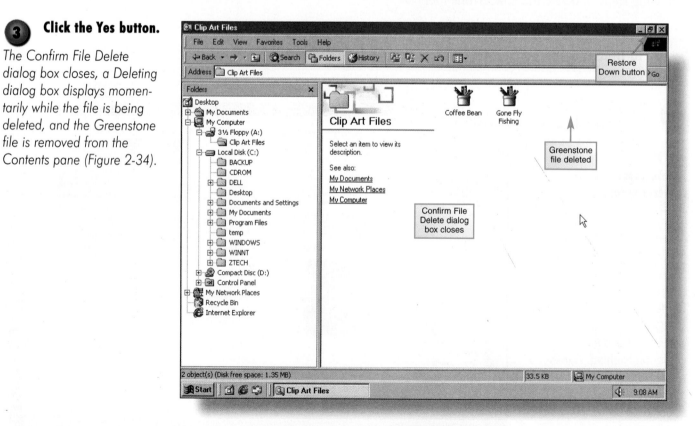

FIGURE 2-34

Deleting a File by Right-Dragging Its Icon

Another method of deleting a file is to right-drag the icon from the Contents pane to the Recycle Bin icon on the desktop. Right-dragging produces a shortcut menu that contains the Move Here command. Currently, the maximized Clip Art Files window occupies the entire desktop. When a window is maximized, you cannot right-drag a file to the Recycle Bin. To allow you to right-drag a file, you first must restore the Clip Art Files window to its original size by clicking the Restore Down button on the title bar. Perform the following steps to delete the Coffee Bean file by right-dragging its icon to the Recycle Bin.

Steps To Delete a File by Right-Dragging

1 **Click the Restore Down button on the Clip Art Files window title bar and then point to the Coffee Bean icon in the Contents pane.**

Windows 2000 restores the Clip Art Files window to its original size and the Maximize button replaces the Restore Down button on the title bar (Figure 2-35). After restoring the window, only the icons in the right panel in the Contents pane display. The left panel in the Contents pane does not display.

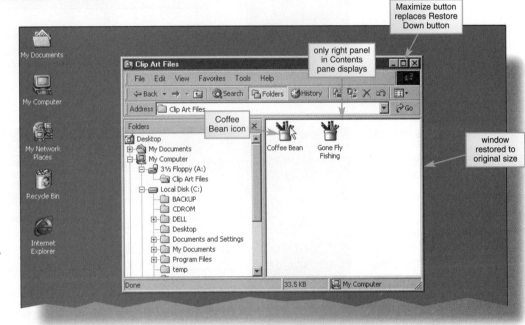

FIGURE 2-35

2 **Right-drag the Coffee Bean icon over the Recycle Bin icon and then point to the Move Here command on the shortcut menu.**

A dimmed Coffee Bean icon displays on top of the Recycle Bin icon on the desktop, a shortcut menu displays, and the Move Here command on the shortcut menu is highlighted (Figure 2-36).

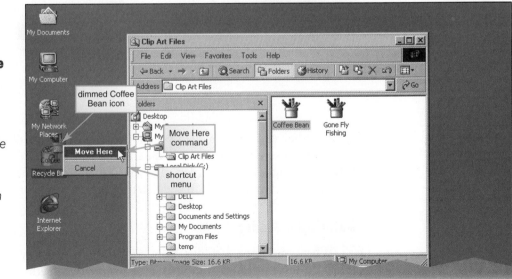

FIGURE 2-36

Click Move Here. When the Confirm File Delete dialog box displays, point to the Yes button.

The Confirm File Delete dialog box displays (Figure 2-37). The dialog box contains the message, Are you sure you want to delete 'Coffee Bean'?, and the Yes and No buttons.

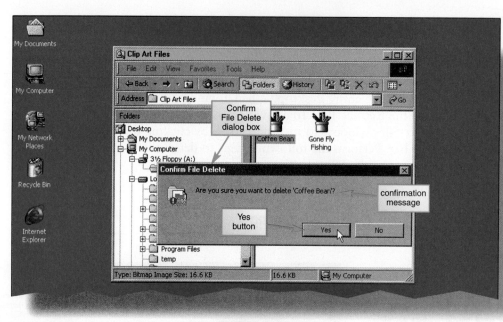

FIGURE 2-37

4 **Click the Yes button.**

The Confirm File Delete dialog box closes, a Deleting dialog box displays momentarily while the file is being deleted, and then the Coffee Bean file is removed from the Contents pane. The Gone Fly Fishing icon displays in the upper-left corner of the Contents pane (Figure 2-38).

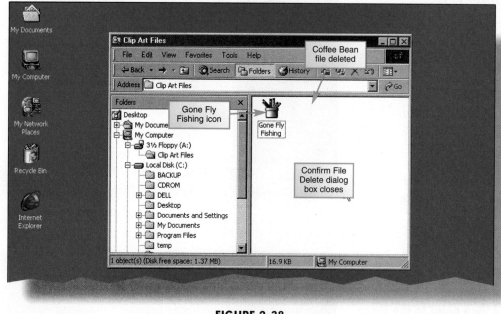

FIGURE 2-38

Whether you delete a file by right-clicking or right-dragging, you also can use the file selection techniques illustrated earlier in this project to delete a group of files. When deleting a group of files, click the Yes button in the Confirm Multiple File Delete dialog box to confirm the deletion of the group of files.

Deleting a Folder

When you delete a folder, Windows 2000 deletes any files or subfolders in the folder. You can delete a folder using the same two methods shown earlier to delete files (right-clicking or right-dragging). Perform the following steps to delete the Clip Art Files folder on drive A by right-dragging its icon to the Recycle Bin.

To Delete a Folder

1 **Point to the Clip Art Files icon in the Folders pane (Figure 2-39).**

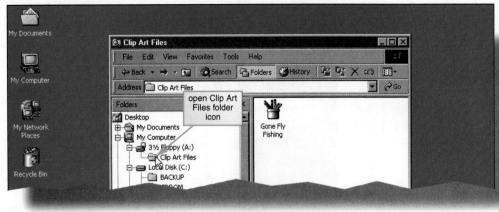

FIGURE 2-39

2 **Right-drag the Clip Art Files icon to the Recycle Bin icon and then point to Move Here on the shortcut menu.**

A dimmed Clip Art Files icon displays on top of the Recycle Bin icon on the desktop, a shortcut menu displays, and the Move Here command on the shortcut menu is highlighted (Figure 2-40).

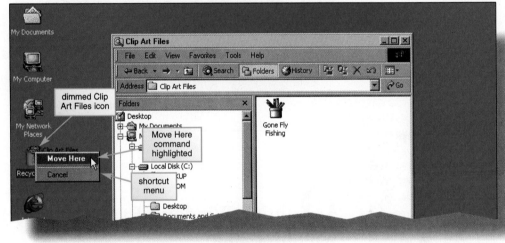

FIGURE 2-40

3 **Click Move Here. When the Confirm Folder Delete dialog box displays, point to the Yes button.**

The Confirm Folder Delete dialog box displays (Figure 2-41). The dialog box contains the message, Are you sure you want to remove the folder 'Clip Art Files' and all its contents?, and the Yes and No command buttons.

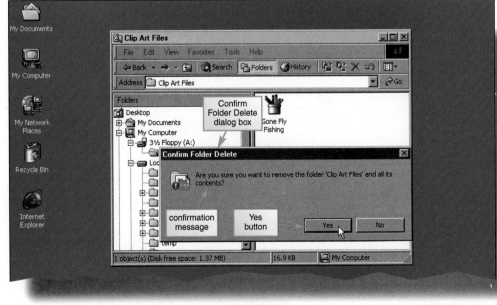

FIGURE 2-41

4 Click the Yes button.

The Confirm Folder Delete dialog box closes, a Deleting dialog box displays momentarily while the folder is being deleted, the Clip Art Files folder is removed from the Folders pane, and a plus sign replaces the minus sign to the left of the 3½ Floppy (A:) icon (Figure 2-42).

5 Remove the floppy disk from drive A.

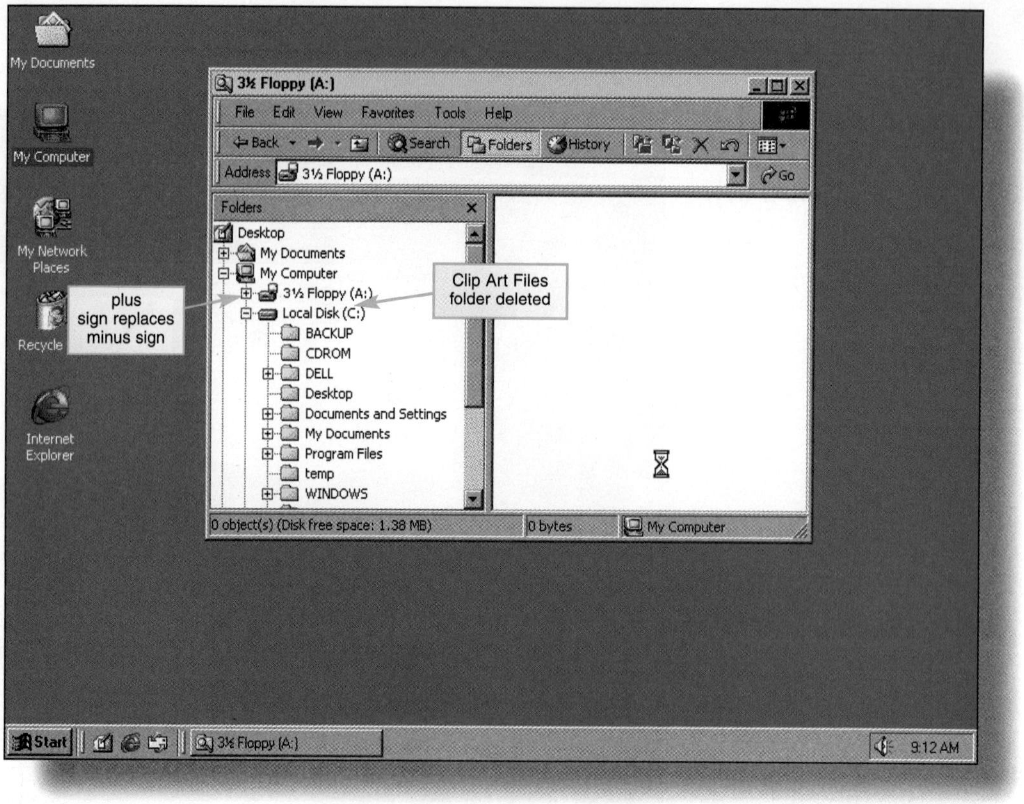

FIGURE 2-42

Other Ways

1. Right-click folder icon, click Delete, click Yes button
2. Drag icon to Recycle Bin, click Yes button
3. Click icon, on File menu click Delete, click Yes button
4. Select icon, press ALT+F, press D, press Y

Quitting Windows Explorer and Shutting Down Windows 2000

After completing your work with Windows Explorer, quit Windows Explorer and then shut down Windows. Perform the following steps to quit Windows Explorer.

TO QUIT AN APPLICATION

1. Point to the Close button in the 3½ Floppy (A:) window.
2. Click the Close button.

Windows 2000 closes the 3½ Floppy (A:) window and quits Windows Explorer.

Shutting Down Windows 2000

After completing work with Windows 2000, you may wish to shut down Windows 2000 using the Shut Down command on the Start menu. If you are sure you want to shut down Windows 2000, perform the following steps. If you do not want to shut down Windows 2000 at this time, read the steps without actually performing them.

TO SHUT DOWN WINDOWS 2000

1 Click the Start button on the taskbar and then point to Shut Down on the Start menu.

2 Click Shut Down. Use the UP ARROW or DOWN ARROW key to display the words, Shut down, in the What do you want the computer to do? box.

3 Click the OK button.

4 Turn off the computer.

Windows 2000 shuts down.

CASE PERSPECTIVE SUMMARY

Your supervisor emphasizes the importance of computer users being able to use Windows 2000 Explorer effectively to control and manage file and folders on their computers. With this in mind, you developed a one-hour class for employees with little computer experience and offered the classes during normal business hours, on alternating weeknights, and on Saturday mornings. Your supervisor was pleased with the results and recommended you for a newly developed networking position in his department.

Project Summary

In this project, you used Windows Explorer to select and copy a group of files, display the contents of a folder, create a folder, expand and collapse a folder, and rename and delete a file and a folder.

What You Should Know

Having completed this project, you now should be able to perform the following tasks:

▶ Collapse a Folder *(WIN 2.11)*
▶ Copy a Group of Files *(WIN 2.20)*
▶ Create a New Folder *(WIN 2.13)*
▶ Delete a File by Right-Clicking *(WIN 2.25)*
▶ Delete a File by Right-Dragging *(WIN 2.27)*
▶ Delete a Folder *(WIN 2.29)*
▶ Display the Contents of a Folder (WIN 2.9, WIN 2.22)
▶ Display the Contents of a Subfolder *(WIN 2.16)*
▶ Expand a Folder (WIN 2.10, WIN 2.15)
▶ Launch Windows Explorer and Maximize Its Window *(WIN 2.6)*
▶ Quit an Application *(WIN 2.30)*
▶ Rename a File *(WIN 2.23)*
▶ Rename a Folder *(WIN 2.24)*
▶ Select a Group of Files *(WIN 2.19)*
▶ Shut Down Windows 2000 *(WIN 2.31)*

Test Your Knowledge

1 True/False

Instructions: Circle T if the statement is true or F if the statement is false.

T F   1. Windows Explorer is an application you can use to organize and work with the files and folders on the computer.

T F   2. Right-clicking the My Computer icon is the only way to launch Windows Explorer.

T F   3. The contents of the selected folder in the Folders pane displays in the Contents pane.

T F   4. To display the contents of drive C on the computer in the Contents pane, click the plus sign to the left of the drive C icon.

T F   5. A folder that is contained within another folder is called a subfolder.

T F   6. To display the contents of a folder, right-click its icon.

T F   7. Collapsing a folder removes the subfolders from the hierarchy of folders in the Folders pane.

T F   8. After you expand a folder, the icons in the Contents pane are always the same as the icons indented and aligned below the folder name in the Folders pane.

T F   9. The source folder is the folder containing the files to be copied.

T F   10. You select a group of files in the Contents pane by pointing to each icon and clicking the mouse button.

2 Multiple Choice

Instructions: Circle the correct response.

1. The Folders pane in the My Computer window contains the _____.
   a. hierarchy of folders   c. source drive
   b. source folder   d. contents of the highlighted folder in the Contents pane
2. The _____ contains the Desktop icon.
   a. Contents pane   c. Folders pane
   b. status bar   d. Standard Buttons toolbar
3. To display the contents of a folder in the Contents pane, _____.
   a. double-click the plus sign to the left of the folder icon
   b. right-click the folder icon in the Folders pane
   c. click the folder icon in the Contents pane
   d. click the folder icon in the Folders pane
4. You _____ the minus sign to the left of a folder icon to expand a folder.
   a. click   c. double-click
   b. drag   d. point to
5. When an expanded folder is collapsed in the Folders pane, _____.
   a. the subfolders in the folder do not display
   b. the My Computer window closes
   c. the computer beeps at you because you cannot perform this activity
   d. the My Computer window displays
6. To select multiple files in the Contents pane, _____.
   a. right-click each file icon
   b. hold down the SHIFT key and then click each file icon you want to select

Test Your Knowledge

   c. hold down the CTRL key and then click each file icon you want to select

   d. hold down the CTRL key and then double-click each file icon you want to select

7. After selecting a group of files, you _____ the group to copy the files to a new folder.

   a. click   c. double-click

   b. right-drag   d. none of the above

8. In _____ format, file and folder icons in the Contents pane are represented by larger icons.

   a. Large Icons   c. List

   b. Small Icons   d. Details

9. You can rename a file or folder by _____ its icon.

   a. right-dragging   c. dragging

   b. double-clicking   d. right-clicking

10. You can delete a file by right-dragging its icon from the Contents pane to the _____ icon on the desktop.

   a. My Computer   c. Recycle Bin

   b. My Network Places   d. My Documents

3 Understanding the My Computer Window

Instructions: In Figure 2-43, arrows point to several items in the My Computer window. Identify the items or objects in the spaces provided.

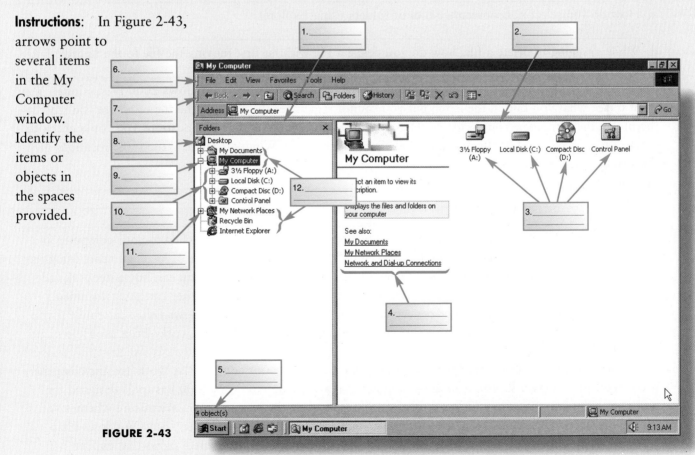

FIGURE 2-43

Use Help

1 Using Windows Help

Instructions: Use Windows Help and a computer to perform the following tasks.

1. If necessary, start Microsoft Windows 2000.
2. Answer the following questions about paths.
   a. What is a path?

   _____

   b. How do you specify a path?

   _____

   _____

   _____

3. In the Windows 2000 window, click the Index tab and then type `windows explorer` in the Type in the keyword to find text box. Answer the following questions about Windows Explorer.
   a. What method is recommended to copy a file or folder?

   _____

   _____

   _____

   b. How do you select consecutive files or folders using Explorer?

   _____

   c. How do you select nonconsecutive files or folders using Explorer?

   _____

   d. While dragging to delete a file, how do you delete a file without first moving the file to the Recycle Bin?

   _____

4. You recently wrote a letter to a friend explaining how to install Microsoft Windows 2000 Professional. You want to see what you said in the letter, but you cannot remember the name of the file or where you stored the file on the computer. You decide to check Windows Help to determine the locations you could check to locate a misplaced file. List the first three locations suggested by Windows Help. Write those locations in the spaces provided.
   Location 1:_____
   Location 2:_____
   Location 3:_____

5. You and your brother each have a computer in your bedroom. A printer is attached to your computer and your brother, whose computer does not have a printer, would like to print some of his documents using the printer attached to your computer. You have heard that for a reasonable cost you can buy a network card and some cable and hook up the two computers on a network. Then, your brother can print documents stored on his computer on the printer connected to your computer. Using Windows Help, determine if you can share your printer. If so, what must you do in Windows 2000 to make this work? Print the Help pages that document your answer.

6. The Windows 2000 Professional operating system is installed on your computer at work and the computer is connected to a network. You read in a computer magazine that Windows 2000 has tools designed for working with files stored on your computer and files stored on the network. You are unsure whether you should use My Briefcase or Offline Files to work with the files on your computer. Using Windows Help, learn about the difference between My Briefcase and Offline Files. Print the Help pages that explain My Briefcase and Offline Files.

1 File and Program Properties

Instructions: Use a computer to perform the following tasks and answer the questions.

1. If necessary, start Microsoft Windows 2000.
2. Right-click the My Computer icon on the desktop and then click Explore on the shortcut menu.
3. Click the plus sign to the left of the Local Disk (C:) icon in the Folders pane.
4. Scroll the Folders pane until the WINNT icon is visible and then click the WINNT icon.
5. If necessary, click the Show Files link in the Contents pane.
6. Scroll the Contents pane until the FeatherTexture icon is visible. If the FeatherTexture icon does not display on your computer, use another Paint icon.
7. Right-click the FeatherTexture icon and then click Properties on the shortcut menu.
8. Answer the following questions about the FeatherTexture file.
   a. What type of file is FeatherTexture? _____
   b. What is the path for the location of the FeatherTexture file? _____
   c. What is the size (in bytes) of the FeatherTexture file? _____
   d. When was the file created? _____
   e. When was the file last modified? _____
   f. When was the file last accessed? _____
9. Click the Cancel button in the FeatherTexture Properties dialog box.
10. Scroll the Contents pane to display the notepad icon.
11. Right-click the notepad icon and then click Properties on the shortcut menu.
12. Answer the following questions:
    a. What type of file is notepad? _____
    b. What is the path of the notepad file? _____
    c. What is the size on disk (in bytes) of the notepad file? _____
    d. What is the file version of the notepad file? _____
    e. What is the file's description? _____
    f. Who is the copyright owner of notepad? _____
    g. For what language is notepad written? _____
13. Click the Cancel button in the notepad Properties dialog box.
14. Close the WINNT window.

2 Windows Explorer

Instructions: Use a computer to perform the following tasks.

1. If necessary, start Microsoft Windows 2000 and then connect to the Internet.
2. Right-click the Start button on the taskbar, click Explore on the shortcut menu, and then maximize the Start Menu window. Your menu may look different.
3. Click the Programs icon in the Folders pane.

(continued)

In the Lab

Windows Explorer *(continued)*

4. Double-click the Internet Explorer icon in the Contents pane to launch the Internet Explorer application.
   a. What is the URL of the Web page that displays on the Address bar in the Microsoft Internet Explorer window? _____
5. Click the URL on the Address bar of the Microsoft Internet Explorer window to select it. Type www.scsite.com and then click the Go button on the Address bar.
6. Right-click the Course Technology logo on the Web page, click Save Picture As on the shortcut menu, and then click the Save button in the Save Picture dialog box to save the image in the My Pictures folder.
7. Click the Close button in the Microsoft Internet Explorer window.
8. Click the plus sign to the left of the My Documents folder icon in the Folders pane.
9. Click the My Pictures icon.
10. Right-click the logo icon in the Contents pane and then click Properties.
    a. What type of file is the logo file? _____
    b. What is the size (in kilobytes) of the file? _____
    c. When was the file last modified? _____
11. Click the Cancel button in the logo Properties dialog box.
12. Insert a formatted floppy disk in drive A of your computer.
13. Right-drag the logo icon onto the 3½ Floppy (A:) icon in the Folders pane. Click Move Here on the shortcut menu.
14. Click the 3½ Floppy (A:) icon in the Folders pane.
    a. Is the logo file stored on the floppy disk? _____
15. Click the Close button in the 3½ Floppy (A:) window.

3 Window Toolbars

Instructions: Use a computer to perform the following tasks.

1. If necessary, start Microsoft Windows 2000.
2. Right-click the My Computer icon on the desktop and then click Explore on the shortcut menu.
3. Expand the Local Disk (C:) icon in the Folders pane.
4. Click the WINNT icon in the Folders pane.
5. If necessary, click the Show Files link in the Contents pane.
6. Click View on the menu bar and then point to Toolbars. If a check mark does not display to the left of the Address Bar command on the Toolbars submenu, click Address Bar. The Address bar displays in the WINNT window.
7. Click the Address box arrow containing the WINNT icon and folder name.
8. Click Control Panel in the Address list.
   a. How did the window change? _____
9. Double-click the WINNT icon in the Folders pane.
   a. What happened? _____

In the Lab

10. In the WINNT window, if the Standard Buttons toolbar does not display, click View on the menu bar, point to Toolbars, and then click Standard Buttons on the Toolbars submenu.

11. Insert a formatted floppy disk in drive A of your computer.

12. If necessary, scroll the Contents pane to display the Soap Bubbles icon. If the Soap Bubbles icon does not display on your computer, use another Paint icon.

13. Select the Soap Bubbles icon and then click the Copy To button on the Standard Buttons toolbar.

14. Click the plus sign to the left of the My Computer icon in the Browse For Folder dialog box, click the 3½ Floppy (A:) icon, and then click the OK button. The Soap Bubbles file is copied to the floppy disk in drive A.

15. Click the Address box arrow and then click the 3½ Floppy (A:) icon in the Address list.

16. The Soap Bubbles icon displays in the Contents pane in the 3½ Floppy (A:) window.

17. Click the Soap Bubbles icon to select the icon, click the Delete button on the Standard Buttons toolbar, and then click the Yes button in the Confirm File Delete dialog box.

18. In the 3½ Floppy (A:) window, return the toolbar status to what it was prior to Step 6.

19. Close the 3½ Floppy (A:) window.

Cases and Places

The difficulty of these case studies varies:
▶ are the least difficult; ▶▶ are more difficult; and ▶▶▶ are the most difficult.

1 ▶ An interesting feature of Windows 2000 is the capability of modifying the view of a window to suit individual preferences. Using Windows Explorer, display the Local Disk (C:) folder in the Contents pane and then experiment with the different commands on the View menu. Describe the effects of the Large Icons, Small Icons, List, and Details commands on the icons in the Contents pane. When using Details view, explain how clicking one of the buttons at the top of the Contents pane (such as Name or Type) changes the window. Finally, specify situations in which you think some of the views you have seen would be most appropriate.

2 ▶ An enormous number of files and folders are stored on your computer's hard disk. Imagine how hard it would be to search through all the folders and files manually to locate a specific file. To simplify the process, Windows 2000 provides the Search command. Click the Start button, point to Search, and then click For Files or Folders on the Search submenu. The Search pane displays in the Search Results window. Use the Help button (a book icon with a question mark on the front cover) in the Search pane to learn more about search options. Try searching for files using the Search pane. Finally, explain how the Search feature works and what options are available for searching for files.

3 ▶▶ Backing up files is an important way to protect data to ensure it is not accidentally lost or destroyed. File backup on a personal computer can use a variety of devices and techniques. Using the Internet, a library, personal computer magazines, and other resources, determine the types of devices used to store backed up data, the schedules, methods, and techniques for backing up data, and the consequences of not backing up data. Write a brief report of your findings.

4 ▶▶ A hard disk must be maintained to remain efficient. This maintenance includes deleting old files, defragmenting a disk so it is not wasteful of space, and from time to time, finding and attempting to correct disk failures. Using the Internet, a library, Windows 2000 Help, and other research facilities, determine the maintenance that you should perform on a hard disk. This includes the type of maintenance, when you should perform it, how long it takes to perform the maintenance, and the risks of not performing the maintenance. Write a brief report on the information you obtain.

5 ▶▶▶ Data stored on disk is one of a company's most valuable assets. If that data were to be stolen, lost, or compromised so it could not be accessed, the company literally could go out of business. Therefore, companies go to great lengths to protect their data. Visit a company or business in your area. Find out how it protects its data against viruses, unauthorized access, and even against such natural disasters as fires, floods, and tornadoes. Prepare a brief report that describes the company's procedures. In your report, point out any areas where you find the company has not protected its data adequately.

Index